131.3
W153L
c.1

Walker, Greta
Living on your own

WITHDRAWN

DATE DUE

Do not remove "date due" card
(25¢ fine if lost)

HACKLEY PUBLIC LIBRARY
MUSKEGON, MICHIGAN

LIVING ON YOUR OWN

BY GRETA WALKER

Designed by Nicholas Krenitsky

FRANKLIN WATTS | NEW YORK | LONDON | 1977

Library of Congress Cataloging in Publication Data

Walker, Greta.
Living on your own.

Includes Index.
SUMMARY: A survival guide for young people living on their own for the first time. Includes tips about finding a job, renting living space, and making decisions.

1. Young adults—United States. 2. Decision-making. 3. Home economics. [1. Decision-making. 2. Home economics] I. Title.
HQ799.7.W33   131'.3   77-8954
ISBN 0-531-00126-1

Copyright © 1977 by Greta Walker
All rights reserved
Printed in the United States of America
5 4 3 2 1

INTRODUCTION
3

CHAPTER 1
Who Are You?
5

CHAPTER 2
City Life
9

CHAPTER 3
Finding A Place
of Your Own
13

CHAPTER 4
Work
33

CHAPTER 5
Problems on the Job
41

CHAPTER 6
Money
47

CHAPTER 7
Food and You
57

CHAPTER 8
Finding Medical Help
67

CHAPTER 9
Values
83

CHAPTER 10
Relationships
89

CHAPTER 11
Protecting Your Rights
101

CHAPTER 12
Extracurricular Activities
109

INDEX
115

What is an adult? Webster's New Collegiate Dictionary defines it as one who is "fully developed and mature." However, one can be fully developed and mature in high school and college and not qualify as an adult in our society. For our purposes we'll define an adult as a person who is financially self-supporting and can make life decisions without consulting a parent.

Being able to vote is not included in this definition, since many states maintain the voting age at twenty-one—a good three years after most of you will be functioning in the adult world. College students are not considered adults in this book. Even though many young people in college are away from home and earning substantial amounts of money, they are still living in a protected environment and are generally not free of parental influence.

This book, then, is for those of you who are not going to college—who have decided to try and make it in the "real world." It will discuss many of the problems you will face as an adult, such as choosing a job, a place to live, roommates, how to handle money, health needs, emotional problems, relationships, ethical problems, job-related problems.

As a young person, living at home, your parents probably made the major decisions in your life, or else they guided you toward some reasonable solutions. But soon you will be on your own, perhaps in a strange city, meeting new people and encountering fresh situations. The evaluations and decisions will have to come from you. The more you know about what you are likely to confront, the more prepared you will be to deal with problems realistically.

This book will attempt to provide guidelines for directing your own life. After all, you gain real freedom by solving your own problems, taking responsibility for your own actions, and by making choices and seeing them through.

Most people learn to function in the adult world by trial and error, and indeed you will probably make your share of mistakes. But perhaps this book can help you cut out a few of the mistakes, and can even offer you things to think about that may lead to positive actions.

It's not easy being an adult, but then it wasn't a bed of roses being a teenager either. The main difference is that now you can call the shots. You owe it to yourself to call them in the best possible way.

1 Who are you?

Before jumping into the adult world with both feet, think a little about yourself and how you will fit into this new life. The more you know about **you** as an individual, the easier it will be to make the correct choices. The following are a few questions you can ask yourself:

Do you get along with your parents? If you do, then you might feel comfortable living at home and staying in your hometown. If you don't, you really should make every effort to find a place of your own and perhaps even think about moving to another city. Make life as easy for yourself as you can. If you are constantly arguing with your parents, you are not going to be able to concentrate fully on yourself.

Are you interested in the jobs that are available in your town? If you are, fine—stick around. If not, take some time to investigate what is available in other cities. You can look through the classified section of out-of-town newspapers. Don't just take the easiest, most comfortable route. Be guided by your real interests, even if it means investigating into unfamiliar territory.

What are your skills? Include your potential skills as well as the skills you already possess. By doing that, you could take a job that utilizes your present expertise, while continuing to develop some new talents.

What are your weaknesses? Best to know them so you don't play into them. You may even decide to strengthen them. The main thing is to be honest with yourself. If you cannot do something, don't pretend you can. Once your deception is discovered, people will lose faith in you.

What are your strengths? You should know them and use them. Just as you must not overrate yourself, you must not underrate yourself. Too often people slight their capabilities. If you know your strengths, you can put them to work for you.

What is your economic situation? Obviously if you are desperate for money you cannot be as choosey as someone who isn't. On the other hand, you can work to earn immediate cash and still plan for future changes.

What are your long-range goals? It is very difficult to look ahead twenty years. However, you should try to think beyond today. Consider the direction in which you are headed. A goal will give you something to aim for, to hope for, to structure your life around. It will affect how you spend and save your money, what extracurricular activities you do, where you live, even who your friends are. Again, be realistic. Your goals have to be achievable. If they are not you will experience nothing but disappointment. In addition, you will waste a good deal of time and money. For example, you may envision yourself as a recording engineer, but if you don't have a natural aptitude for math and electronics, forget it. The competition is fierce, and you would do better to aim for something that will utilize your strengths. Another example is modeling—a very glamorous profession to be sure, but if you don't fit the physical requirements you do not stand a chance. Look to your talents to guide you, not to your fantasies.

Once you start asking yourself who you are, you will probably think of many more questions than are listed here. That is good because you want to avoid making decisions just because they are expected of you, or because your best friend is doing them. You want to make decisions that are right for you. This is especially necessary in order to withstand opposition; parents and friends may feel you are wrong in choosing a certain occupation or moving to a certain town, or pursuing a particular activity. If you are strong in your conviction, if you have made a realistic decision based on what you know about your own capacities, you won't be diverted from your goal by opposing voices.

So start out your adulthood by getting to know the most important person in your life—you.

2
City Life

Big city living is not for everyone. But frequently you must choose to live in a large metropolis such as Detroit, Chicago, or New York, because that is where the jobs are. For some of you the city will be a great adventure, for others a place to endure until you can save enough money to get out. Whatever your feelings, city dwelling will be easier if you have some idea of how to cope with it.

Many of you may be fearful about the safety of city life. There's no question that the crime rate is higher in crowded areas with a diverse population and a high degree of poverty. Nevertheless, if you take the necessary precautions, you can live in relative safety in any of our large cities.

The neighborhood you choose is important. All cities have sections that are more prone to burglaries and muggings than others. You will be wise to check out neighborhoods before beginning the search for a place to live. Ask the advice of several people because some folks are more fearful than others. They may categorize a neighborhood as unsafe when it is actually quite all right. For example, in Manhattan there are Eastsiders who are nervous about even going to the West Side, much less living there. Those fears are absurd since there are thousands of people living happily and safely, and at lower rents, in West-Side apartments. On the other hand, some areas on the West Side are safer than others and people looking for apartments should be aware of them.

Finding a safe building is also important. Apartment houses with an alert doorman are usually safer than unattended buildings. However, even a building that has no doorman can be well protected if the tenants are very careful about who is allowed into the building (in these houses the tenants control the main door of the house by a buzzer system). Check with the tenants. In some cases tenants will contribute money to hire a guard for the building. That's an excellent crime deterrent.

No matter how safe your building, you will have to practice safety rules in your own apartment. Your front door—and back door if you have one—should always be locked. The small-town hospitality of the unlocked door is not appropriate in a large city. Your locks should be of the best quality—pick resistant. If your landlord will not provide more than a conventional lock, it is worth the money to have a locksmith install a second more secure device. Windows near fire escapes need guards, and if you live on the ground floor you will need protective guards on all windows (they will probably already be installed). Your front door will have a peephole and you should use it before opening the door to **anyone.**

The following are some do's and don'ts for city living:

Don't let strangers into your apartment.

Leave a spare set of keys with a neighbor or your superintendent in case you lock yourself out.

Don't leave a lot of money in the house.

Don't carry a great deal of money on the street.

Do make sure you carry some money. Tuck a $10 bill in your wallet and forget about it.

If you're a woman living alone **don't** advertise it. List yourself as J. Smith in the telephone book instead of Jane Smith. Do the same on your mailbox and apartment building tenant list.

Don't bring strange men home.

Despite the need for safety precautions, there are enormous benefits from city life. All major cities have wonderful museums, an abundance of movies, restaurants with food from every country in the world, concerts of classical and rock music, great places to hear jazz, bookstores, libraries, art galleries, and boutiques that sell everything. Many facilities are free or very inexpensive. Even if you cannot wait to leave, take advantage of what is good.

Cities are also great places for walking. You are not so dependent on automobiles as in smaller communities, and if you choose to, you can get to and from your destinations by using your legs—a very practical way to get exercise. If walking is not your style, subways and buses are efficient and fast, though not always clean.

Again regarding safety, you needn't be afraid of going about the city as long as you're aware that you don't go to certain areas at certain times of night. Other than that, cities are marvelous after dark. There are so many things to do, and there are always people out walking around. In fact cities are fun because of the great number of people who throng the avenues day and night. You will see individuals of all colors, speaking a variety of languages. Clothing is eclectic with everything from saris worn by handsome Indian women, to jeans on all types of young people, to the latest fashions on the city's trend-setters. There are smells and sounds and colors that you would never find in a little town or a smaller city—a veritable feast for the senses.

So if the city is where you are headed, come prepared to take precautions, but also to enjoy.

Whether your first step is finding a place to live or looking for a job will depend on your individual situation. Those of you who want to live at home, or in your hometown, will probably give first priority to finding work. Those of you moving to other cities must find a place to live before you start the rounds of employment agencies.

Your best bet, if you are going to a strange city, is to get a room at a residence hall or a YMCA or YWCA (some towns have YMHAs and YWHAs). If you know someone in town you may be able to stay with them for awhile. The point is not to commit yourself to an apartment before you know the city and before you feel financially secure. Once you are settled with a two- or three-year lease, it is difficult to pull up stakes and move on. So get some comfortable temporary quarters and allow yourself time to become familiar with your new environment.

Ideally you should have a few thousand dollars saved (although most of you probably don't). Money in the bank is a great way to prevent becoming frantic about employment. In addition, you're not in the position of having to take from anyone until you find a regular income. The last point is very important. In a rash moment friends may say, "Stay with us as long as you want." They really want to help but, as so often is the case, it is harder to live with someone who isn't paying his or her share of food and rent, than it is to be friends. You take them up on their offer and two weeks later (or less) resentment sets in, and you are clearly the unwanted, nonpaying guest. So there you are, short of cash, out of work, and dependent on hostile roommates. Try to avoid that situation at all costs. The more independence you have, the easier your adult life will be.

Once you have found temporary lodgings you can begin the job hunt (how you go about that will be discussed in Chapter 4). When you feel secure in your work situation you can start looking for a place of your own.

Having one's own apartment for the first time is an exhilirating experience. It may only be one large room, but it's all yours to decorate as you like, to accommodate your particular lifestyle, to serve as a retreat when you want some privacy. Take time to select your living place. Decide whether you want to live alone or share with a roommate. What neighborhood suits you best? What transportation facilities do you need? How many rooms do you require? What can you afford to pay? (One quarter of your monthly salary has been suggested by economists.) You may have to compromise on some points. But at least you will start out with a clear idea of what you need instead of going aimlessly from one place to another.

In small towns, apartment hunting offers limited choices, so your task will be easier. In larger cities, finding a place to live is often frightening and confusing. You may come up against unscrupulous real estate agents, landlords, and building superintendents. The more you are prepared for them the less likely it is you will be one of their victims, but more about this later.

If you feel that for financial and/or emotional reasons you must have a roommate, choose wisely. Your best friend could turn into your worst enemy after a month of living together. It is one thing to see each other socially, it is another to share a refrigerator, bathroom, expenses, and household decisions. As much as possible, talk to each other about personal needs and idiosyncracies before making a commitment. Once you have decided to become roommates, you could set up a time each month (or every couple of weeks) to discuss your gripes and try and iron them out. Unspoken resentments only get worse.

Lacking friends in the city, some of you will find roommates through the classified section of the local newspaper. Here's a sample from **The New York Times:**

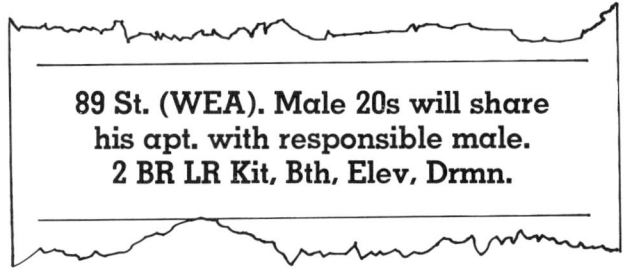

89 St. (WEA). Male 20s will share his apt. with responsible male. 2 BR LR Kit, Bth, Elev, Drmn.

That ad tells you several things: the neighborhood—89th street at West End Avenue, that a young male roommate is wanted, that the apartment has two bedrooms (you will have a room of your own), a living room, kitchen, bathroom (only one so you will share), an elevator, and a doorman. The ad also gives a phone number which I haven't included. It doesn't give the rent.

You can find out the rent over the phone, and you can also ask a few questions about the person who has the apartment: What kind of work does he do? What hours does he keep? Does he like his privacy, and will he allow you some? If the answers satisfy you, then you can go and look at the apartment (if you feel uncomfortable asking so many questions on the phone, you can save them until you meet the person. The reason for the telephone inquiries is to save you an unnecessary trip).

Be prepared to ask your prospective roommate for character references and be prepared to offer some of your own. His boss would be a good reference. You could also talk to his former roommate or to a couple of his neighbors. Check whether the apartment is kept in a way that would be comfortable to you. Is the man someone with whom you feel at ease? Of course you can not know everything until you have lived with someone, but you can find out a good deal.

Listen to your own instincts, even if you are lacking facts. For example, if you feel uneasy about the person, and you're not sure why, respect your feelings. Those little flashes we get about people often turn out to be justified. If you want to take time to think about moving in, don't allow yourself to be pressured into making a snap judgment. This is a big decision and shouldn't be hastily made. He may tell you that if you don't take it immediately you will lose out. Better to lose out than to rush things. There will be other apartments.

> **80E UNBELIEVABLE 3 RM $197**
> immac mod bldg rent controlled apt
> +C 18' LR sep BR No Fee Phone number

The above New York City ad tells you the apartment is in the east eighties (a nice neighborhood), that it is a fantastic three-room apartment for $197.00 a month (a reasonable rent for that neighborhood). It goes on to say that it is in an immaculate modern building (you don't have to worry about cockroaches) and that the apartment is rent controlled (the rent will stay at a relatively low level). In addition, there are several closets (+C), an eighteen-foot living room (a nice size room), and a separate bedroom. There is no fee to pay. Most rental agents charge the equivalent of one month's rent as their fee. So the last item means the apartment is probably not being advertised by a broker, but by a landlord.

When you decide to take an apartment, either alone or with another person, you are often confronted with a renting agent. This individual has been designated by the landlord to find someone suitable as a tenant for the empty apartment. What this means for you is one month's rent paid to the agent (the fee), one month's rent paid to the landlord, and a deposit of one month's rent paid to the landlord that will be refunded when you move out (the landlord is obliged to pay you interest on that deposit, but often if you don't remind him or her you won't get it). That means, if your rent is $200 a month, you will have to lay out $600 before you even move into your new home. If there is no fee, you will only have to pay the rent and the deposit (called one month's "security" against your failing to pay your rent).

Sometimes people find apartments by querying superintendents of a building, thus bypassing the rental agent's fee. However, superintendents usually expect a financial reward for their help. This could be as much as a month's rent, so you have not saved anything. Don't give the superintendent money before he or she actually gets you the apartment. Make no deposits with a super on the basis of a promise to help you. This is usually money down the drain.

Do not go to rental agents who demand $25 or $30 for sending you to look at apartments. They will take your money and will give you a list of apartments that are either uninhabitable or where no one is ever home when you call or go. Reputable agents only take the fee when you rent the apartment.

When you go to talk to the landlord or renting agent you should look as neat and responsible as possible. The landlord's main concern is that he or she will get a tenant who will maintain the apartment properly, and will be able to pay the rent. A nice appearance is very reassuring. If you have a job and a bank account, that assures the landlord that you are financially reliable.

Should you feel you are being turned down on an apartment because you belong to a particular ethnic group, or because you are part of a group of women who want to share a place (sometimes two or more women are turned down for a large apartment because they are suspected of being call girls), or because you are single, you can do something about it.

What usually happens in cases of discrimination is that the landlord or agent will tell you the apartment is available over the phone, then when you come to the apartment or the office, and it becomes apparent that you are black or Hispanic or oriental, or that several women want the apartment, or that you are an unmarried woman, you are told there was a mistake and the apartment is already rented. This is illegal and you can call the city agency that deals with discrimination. Check your telephone directory for a human rights commission, or call information and tell them you want to contact an agency that fights discrimination in housing.

If you want the apartment, the agency will do something on your behalf. However, as in all legal proceedings, these things can be time consuming and slow moving. If you are desperate to find something quickly, you may not want to be bothered, but if you can afford to wait, and you like the apartment a lot, it is a good idea to pursue the issue—first, because landlords shouldn't be allowed to get away with these tactics, and second, because you could very well end up with your dream apartment.

When you find an apartment you want to take, check out the building with the neighbors: How is the service? Are there problems and delays about getting things fixed? If there is an elevator, does it break down frequently? Is it a safe building? Not only are you obtaining information, but you are getting to meet the neighbors. It gives you a chance to find out if these are people you would enjoy living near. Are there a great many elderly people who might be disturbed by your rock records and your late parties? Do the neighbors seem happy living in this building? If the tenants of your prospective home haven't moved out yet, you can query them about why they are moving—does it have anything to do with not liking the apartment or the building or the neighbors?

Finally! You've seen everything, talked to everyone, thought things through, and (gulp) you'll take it. The next step is signing a lease. Some places don't offer a lease, but if you feel more comfortable with something in writing, you could ask for a letter of agreement.

A lease is a contract between you and the landlord setting down the terms of your relationship for a period of one, two, or three years. At the end of that period you will sign a new lease and your rent will probably increase. Read your lease carefully before signing it: Does it say the landlord will paint the apartment before you move in? It should. Are there things you want fixed that are not listed in the lease? You can ask to have them added. Is there a sublet clause that says you can rent your apartment to someone else if you have to go away for several months? Not all landlords will allow this but you can ask for it if you think you'll need it. In an emergency, can you break your lease? This is the time to ask questions about anything that bothers you in the contract. Don't be afraid to inquire about sections you don't understand. Whenever you sign a legal document, you should understand it completely.

Once you and the landlord have signed the lease, the apartment is yours. You now have a place of your own.

In Witness Wh[ereof...]
year first above written.

Witness for Landlord:
Ego

Witness for Tenant:
Robert

Agreem[ent]
JOSEPH
party of the first part
NICHOLAS
Witnesseth:
Apartment
known as 227 Ce[ntral...]
York, for the term of
th[...]

Apartment

Premises

Tenant

Expires

STANDARD FORM OF APARTMENT

 **Lease**

Management Division
The Real Estate Board of New York, Inc.
Copyright 1942. All Rights Reserved.
Reproduction in whole or in part prohibited.

FEATHERING YOUR NEST

If you are fortunate enough to find an apartment completely furnished from the bed to the pots and pans, you will not have to think about what to put into your new home. The chances are, however, that even if you have a furnished place, you will find that you are missing the perfect frying pan, or you would like to put up your own curtains, or you simply must have a new mattress on the bed.

Before you go off on a shopping spree, take the time to think about what things you really need, and the best places to buy them.

When it comes to major pieces of furniture, such as sofas, upholstered chairs, and beds, department stores are your best bet. They usually have a larger selection, and should you have trouble with a purchase, you will have less of a hassle getting service or your money back if you are dealing with a large company. Try to do your shopping when the store is having a sale, for then you can get quality merchandise at a substantial savings. And you do want quality on certain items.

For example, don't try to cut corners when you buy a mattress—buy a good one on sale, but don't buy an inferior brand. A good firm mattress will last many years and will keep you from developing all the aches and pains that come from uncomfortable sleep.

On the other hand you can skimp on the frame. You don't need a fancy headboard or an expensive box spring. You will do very well with a simple wooden base on which to place your mattress. You can build it yourself out of plywood, and you can make it as low or as high as you wish. If you are really resourceful, you can construct the base with a storage compartment in which to keep blankets, sleeping bags, and so forth.

If your apartment is only one room, and your bed

has to serve as a sofa, you might want to consider a hi-riser rather than a convertible couch. They are much less expensive, can open up to be a double bed or two single beds, and they will be more adaptable in the future when you move to larger quarters. Naturally, a twin bed can also serve as a sofa by adding some bolsters, a good looking cover, and some throw pillows.

Don't be afraid to test furniture when you go to buy it:

Lie on a mattress to make sure it suits your back.

Sit on chairs and couches and wiggle around to see if they are good and firm. Make sure the cushions are well-padded. You don't want to feel springs when you are sitting.

Does the fabric look durable on upholstered pieces? Is it treated so that spills wipe off easily? It should be. You don't want to have to slipcover an upholstered piece within a year.

Do you like the color and design of the fabric? You take a great risk if you buy an upholstered piece that you feel half-hearted about. Stuffed chairs and sofas are expensive. And you could find yourself living with something you don't like for a **long** time because you cannot afford to replace it. When in doubt—wait! But if you decide to buy, it is a good idea to take a small color drawing of your room with you, or take swatches of fabric, to refer to if you are coordinating colors. Don't rely on your memory.

Don't be afraid to ask questions of the salesperson if you have any doubts about a piece.

Above all, don't let a salesperson talk you into something when you're feeling uncertain. These purchases are too important to buy quickly, or at someone else's urging.

When it comes to chests, wooden chairs, and tables, you will probably do better at a used-furniture store, or even at the Salvation Army. You can often pick up handsome pieces that are in good condition. Sometimes the finish is in poor condition, but with a little sanding and waxing you can end up with a great-looking chest, chair, or table that not only did not cost very much, but is likely to grow in value as the years go by. For example, folks who bought round oak tables in the 1960s for $65, now find they are worth $200 and up.

Used furniture should be given just as careful a scrutiny as new department store pieces:

Are legs of chairs and tables well braced so the pieces don't wobble? Don't buy anything that appears to be rickety.

Do the drawers of chests have secure joints?

Do drawers slide in and out easily?

Is the wood still in good condition, or is it splintering? Avoid the latter.

If there are any veneered parts, are they holding fast or are they beginning to peel off? If they are peeling, pass them by unless the wood underneath is attractive enough to stand on it's own.

How much work will be involved to make the piece look good? Do you want to put in all that labor? No sense buying something that will make you feel overburdened.

The used-furniture dealer can probably give you some tips on refinishing, but you are better off in picking up a book on the subject before you even go shopping. You will find a great variety in the paperback section of any bookstore, or at the library.

Unpainted furniture from department stores or from small lumber shops can also be fixed up to look quite nice. But the design of most of it is fairly square and unimaginative. And it isn't all that inexpensive.

Bookcases, of course, you can build yourself. One way is with metal strips and brackets. This method is particularly good because you can vary the spaces between shelves; they don't look as heavy as standard bookcases in a small room; and if you get bored with one arrangement you can easily rearrange them. Cheap pine boards, either stained or painted, are perfect for the shelves.

Just remember:

Use graph paper to design your shelf arrangement before having the metal strips and the boards cut to size.

Be sure to get the proper screws for putting up the strips, or your beautiful shelves will come toppling down.

When the strips begin to tarnish, they can be painted the color of the walls.

Fixing up an apartment does not stop with furniture. You will need linens and kitchen equipment.

When it comes to linens—sheets and towels—go back to the department stores. That is where you will find the best values. Stores frequently feature irregulars—top-quality sheets and towels that have small

DECORATIONS FOR DRESSERS

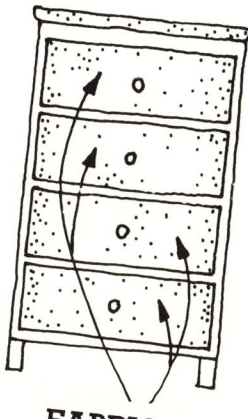

FABRIC COVERED

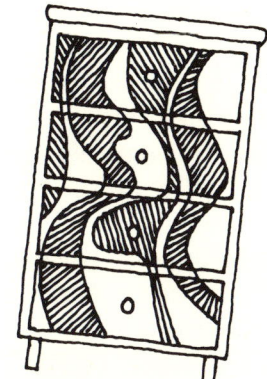

FREE HAND DESIGN

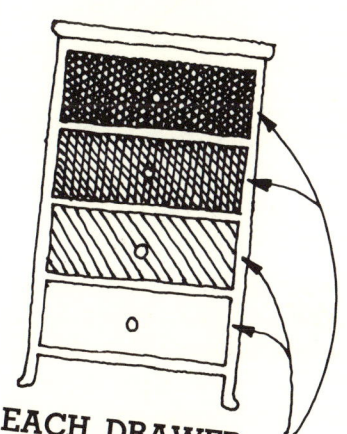

EACH DRAWER A DIFFERENT COLOR

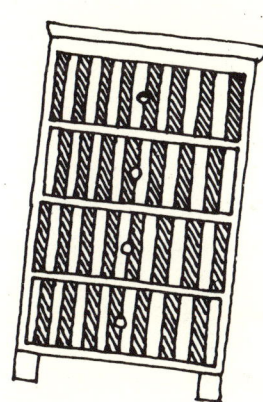

PAINTED STRIPES OR STRIPES OF COLORED TAPE

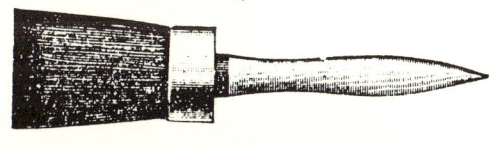

flaws—for half the price. These are wonderful buys. You will get really beautiful merchandise that will last a long time for very little money. However, check the small flaws—usually some threads that are sticking out or some imperfect stitching—to see that the small flaw will not ultimately unravel and become a big one.

By the way, sheets and towels are very versatile and can be used decoratively outside the bedroom and bathroom:

- Patterned sheets make lovely curtains. They look especially attractive when they match the sheets and pillow cases on your bed.
- Table cloths can be made from sheets. Cut them round for a round table or keep them as they are for a long rectangular table.
- A round plywood table in the living room can be covered with a patterned sheet that is cut in a circle and reaches to the floor.
- Hand towels, or terry-cloth dish towels can become bathroom curtains. Hang them café style with clip-on rings.

When you buy kitchen equipment—pots and pans, and so forth—if possible, get good quality utensils. They literally never wear out so you have made a very sound investment. If you live in a town that has a place that specializes in kitchenware, go when they are having a sale. Otherwise try the department stores, also at sale time.

Silverware and dishes can be very inexpensive. Simple white or glass dishes are serviceable, good looking and cheap. Stainless steel flatware is well designed and not at all costly.

Should you buy a toaster or a blender, go for the name brands that you can rely on.

An excellent guide for buying anything from household equipment to automobiles to gardening tools is **Consumer Reports.** It is a monthly magazine—available by subscription only or at the library—that tests products and then lists them according to performance, durability, and price.

Once you have put the essentials into your apartment, you will no doubt begin to think of decorative touches. Well, they need not be expensive, especially if you are willing to get involved in do-it-yourself projects:

- Stunning linoleum can be laid by you in self-sticking squares.
- Hanging your own wallpaper is much easier than you think, especially if you get the kind with an adhesive backing that does not require glue.
- Plants at the window, hanging from ceiling hooks or wall brackets, make wonderful decorations. Buy your plants small and watch them become huge and exotic.
- Learn to propogate plants. A $3.00 spider plant will ultimately provide you with six rooms full of foliage, as well as gift plants to take to friends.
- Growing flowering plants under fluorescent lights adds great beauty to a room and is fun.
- Use plastic cubes for framing pictures. They are marvelously inexpensive and when you are bored with one picture, you can easily take it out and replace it with another.
- Frames picked up at used-furniture shops are not very costly either, and some of them are quite beautiful.
- Brightly colored posters can really make a room. A framing shop will affix a heavy backing to the poster so it will not curl, but even without a backing posters are terrific.
- Making your own throw pillows is another way to enliven a room.

Decorating an apartment, like everything else, is not forever. Things you consider perfect now may be unappealing to you five years hence, and even the sturdiest fabrics in time begin to fade. So bear this in mind as you go about your decorating chores. Don't invest everything you have in your first attempt at furnishing. As you change and grow, so will your lifestyle and your taste. This is only the beginning.

HOW TO FIX IT

Every home needs a tool chest. You do not need to rush out and buy an expensive, fully equipped set of tools. You can pick up the basic supplies you need at any reasonably well-stocked neighborhood hardware store.

You need a carpenter's claw hammer (they come in different weights so be sure to select one that feels comfortable in your hand); a tack hammer (this is handy for small light nails, which should be most of what you will find yourself nailing); screw drivers (buy at least two sizes, a long handled one and a short handled one). Plan to acquire a Phillips screw driver. They are not expensive, and some types of screws cannot be removed without one. You will also need at least one pair of pliers. Buy nails and screws of several sizes and thicknesses. (As strange as it may seem, these are expensive, and are often sold individually. Buy only what you need.) A small can of machine oil, a steel tape measure, a flashlight with batteries that work, and a roll of friction tape should complete your basic needs. You can buy other items as you need them.

REPAIRS YOU CAN HANDLE

Fix rattling windows
Glueing almost anything glueable
Painting rooms
Painting furniture
Patching small areas of plaster or masonry
Changing fuses; rewiring small appliances; putting new plugs on wires
Minor plumbing chores such as unstopping sinks or toilets
Replacing small panes of window glass
Resetting loose tiles; filling cracks around tubs or sinks

REPAIRS YOU SHOULD NOT ATTEMPT

Fixing major appliances such as television sets or stoves
Major electrical wiring such as wires in walls
Hanging heavy mirrors
Placing large sheets of glass in windows
Don't do anything that requires scaffolding
To be on the safe side, check with your landlord before attempting any repair that you have doubts about.

WHAT YOU SHOULD DO IN A COMMUNITY EMERGENCY

ELECTRICITY

Shut off individual appliances but **don't** pull the main switch **unless** there is danger of flooding. You may need your lights or radio or a hot plate. **But** if the area around the main switch is already flooded, **keep away from it!**

  If fuses blow or circuit breakers operate, **don't** try to fix them. Wait for the electric company to do the job. **Don't** touch **any** fallen wires.

WATER

Don't shut off your water unless pipes are broken. You may need it to put out small fires, or for sanitary use.

  Don't draw lots of water for "emergency" use. This reduces the pressure in the water mains so fire fighting equipment can't operate. You can always use the water in your water heater for drinking or cooking.

GAS

Shut off the appliances just as you do when you are not using them. **Don't** shut off appliances like the furnace or the water heater. **Don't** shut off the gas at the meter unless you receive official instructions to do so. Then follow the instructions exactly.

  Don't try to turn the gas on at the meter yourself. Wait for the utility company to come.

  Don't light matches or turn on electric switches in the area of any leak. Get the utility company as soon as possible.

MAINTENANCE OF A MATTRESS

1

Turn your mattress at least once a month. Reverse head and foot as well as top and bottom. This will help an innerspring mattress last longer.

2

Air your mattress. (A foam rubber mattress should not be left in the hot sun.)

3

Protect your mattress from stains by using a plastic or rubberized cover under your bottom sheet.

4

Vacuum your mattress on both sides about once a month.

5

Dry cleaning fluids should not be used to clean foam rubber mattresses.

6

Sitting on the edge of your bed will, in time, break down the walls of your mattress.

This label appears on a piece of upholstered furniture to identify some of the construction materials used.

No. 3
UNDER PENALTY OF LAW
THIS TAG NOT TO BE REMOVED
EXCEPT BY THE CONSUMER

ALL NEW MATERIAL CONSISTING OF	
LATEX FOAM RUBBER	25%
POLYESTER FIBERS	30%
POLYURETHANE FOAM	20%
CEMENTED SHREDDED URETHANE FOAM	25%

LIC. NO. STATE 000

This article is made in compliance with an Act of the Dist. of Columbia approved July 3, 1926; Kansas approved March 1923; Minn. approved April 24, 1929; N.J. revised statutes 26; 10-6 to 18. La. Act 467-1948..	CERTIFICATION IS MADE BY THE MANUFACTURER THAT THE MATERIALS IN THIS ARTICLE ARE DESCRIBED IN ACCORDANCE WITH LAW.

MADE BY
COMPANY, INC.

WINDOW FRAMES

If your window has no curtain or shade, or if your curtains don't cover the window frame, or if you are using window shades only, you can decorate the frame in some of these ways:

1
Paint the frame in a color that matches your room. Use a narrow roller (there's one in your hardware store that is sold just for this particular job). Protect the glass by using masking tape. If you happen to get paint on the window, wait until it is thoroughly dry and then scrape it off with a single-edge razor blade or paint scraper.

2
Colored tapes can be attached around window frame. Use wide tapes, or narrow tapes of different colors.

3
Apply decorative trim, ribbon, or rope with glue.

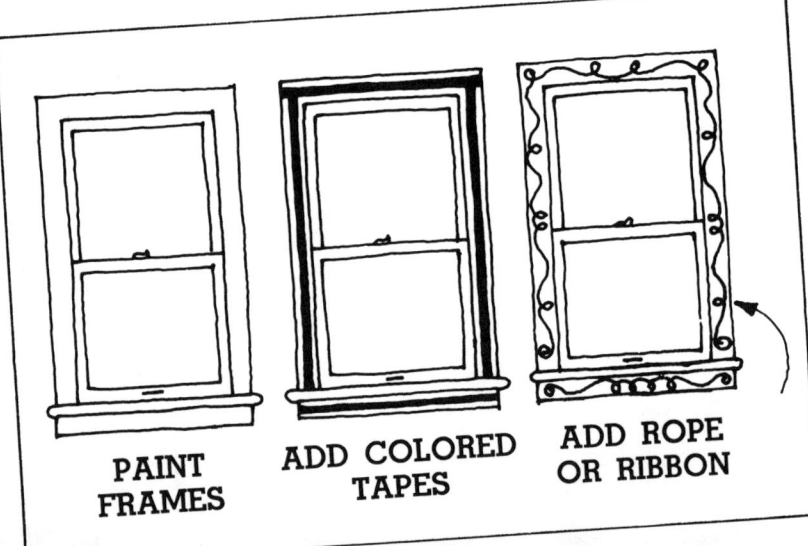

PAINT FRAMES   ADD COLORED TAPES   ADD ROPE OR RIBBON

There is no way to avoid work. Unless you have an independent income, or someone will support you, you will have to earn a living. If you accept that right from the start, you will come to terms with the way you will earn a living much more quickly. Doing a job for money will occupy a large percentage of your life. Try to find a career that will give you pleasure and upward mobility over a period of years.

Women should be especially conscious of this advice. Too often young women use work as a stopgap between high school and marriage. The idea is to keep themselves afloat until Mr. Right comes along. Then they can marry and have children. Being a wife and mother is a perfectly valid occupation, but no woman should allow it to cancel out her ability to be self-supporting. Life plays too many tricks. Mr. Right doesn't come along. Mr. Right doesn't earn enough to support the family and you have to work. You find housewifery boring and you want to work but you have no skills. The marriage doesn't last and you have to go back to work. Your children grow up and don't need you so much. You must be prepared.

Work is one of the few things you can have as your own—always. Lovers, husbands, and children may leave you but your work will stay with you, growing and getting better. Making money gives you power in our society. You do not have to be dependent on others. You won't feel compelled to stay in an unhappy relationship because you can't support yourself. You can take care of your own needs. As a married woman you can be an equal financial partner with equal say about how the family money is spent.

While looking for a permanent job, you can usually earn some money by doing temporary work. Typing, clerking, waiting tables, and so forth, are ways of paying the bills until you have a full-time position you enjoy. In fact, temporary work—especially for men and women who have clerical skills—can be a way of exploring possible full-time jobs. Temporary services will send you to a variety of offices and you can try out different businesses while earning money. Some services even have what they call "Temp to Perm," a way for an employee to try out a job without a commitment from the temporary worker or the employer. After several weeks, if a decision is made in favor of the job, it becomes permanent.

Whatever you do, try not to let yourself get into desperate financial straits. If you do you may take a permanent job that is not to your liking because it enables you to pay your bills.

Think carefully about the kind of career you have in mind. Sometimes it is to your advantage to start out in a lower paying job that offers training for and advancement to more complicated work than to take a higher paying position that goes nowhere.

Of course there is always the chance that an employer will promise to train you and then never fulfill the promise. Your only recourse in that case is to remind him or her that training was part of the bargain. If after a year there is no evidence that you are ever going to learn anything more in this position, start looking for another job. Even if your employer urges you to stay, regaling you with visions of future possibilities, you should be very skeptical. Tell him or her you want the training **now** or you leave. No sense hanging around when you could be upwardly mobile elsewhere.

Since none of you have held full-time jobs in the past, you will not have to compose a résumé. However, interviewers will ask you about part-time jobs you held while in high school, such as baby sitting, clerking in a local store, delivering papers, and so forth. You should be prepared to list the jobs with the names and addresses of your employers. You should also come equipped with the name and address of a character reference—someone who has known you for a number of years and who will say that you are honest and reliable. Do not forget to mention any special skills or accomplishments. You might even make a written list to carry with you to interviews.

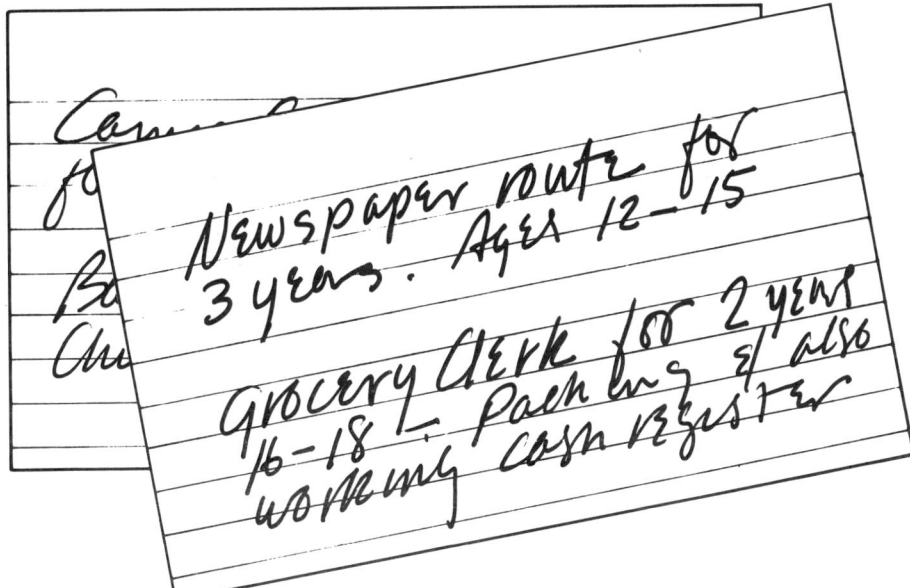

Be sure to dress neatly for your appointments. Each city and each employer has its own dress code, but all employers do stress good grooming and cleanliness. Although jeans are permitted in many jobs, it is a good idea not to wear them to an interview. Women should stick to regular pants or skirts and men can wear slacks and a jacket (if you're going for an office job you should wear a tie). If you notice that others are much more casually dressed and that casual clothes seem to be quite acceptable, you can be more informal on your next day of appointments.

Looking for work, as everyone knows, is no fun. As the hopeful employee you often must go through uncomfortable interviews that leave you wondering anxiously if you made a terrible fool of yourself. It needn't be so horrifying if you can allow yourself to be as natural as possible (you never appear foolish by just being yourself). Do not try to project yourself into some person you think they are looking for. It doesn't work. Be as straightforward and honest as you can. If you are good at certain things don't be afraid to say so. If you can not do something, but feel sure you could easily learn it on the job, let the interviewer know that too. Being nervous is natural—even very sophisticated people become ill at ease in these situations.

You may ask questions—in fact you should find out as much as you can about the job in order to know if you really want it. The purpose of an interview is to allow both parties to obtain information. If the person interviewing you will be your boss, figure out if you could take orders from that man or woman. Do you like the work facilities? What are the health benefits? How long a vacation will you get? How strict are working conditions? Will someone be looking over your shoulder or will you be given relative freedom? Any area of importance to you should be explored.

Some interviews will go through two stages—first an interview with an employment agency and then with the prospective employer. The following is a sample ad from an employment agency. The name of the agency is fictitious, as is the address, but the message in the ad is exactly as it appeared in the classified section of a large city newspaper:

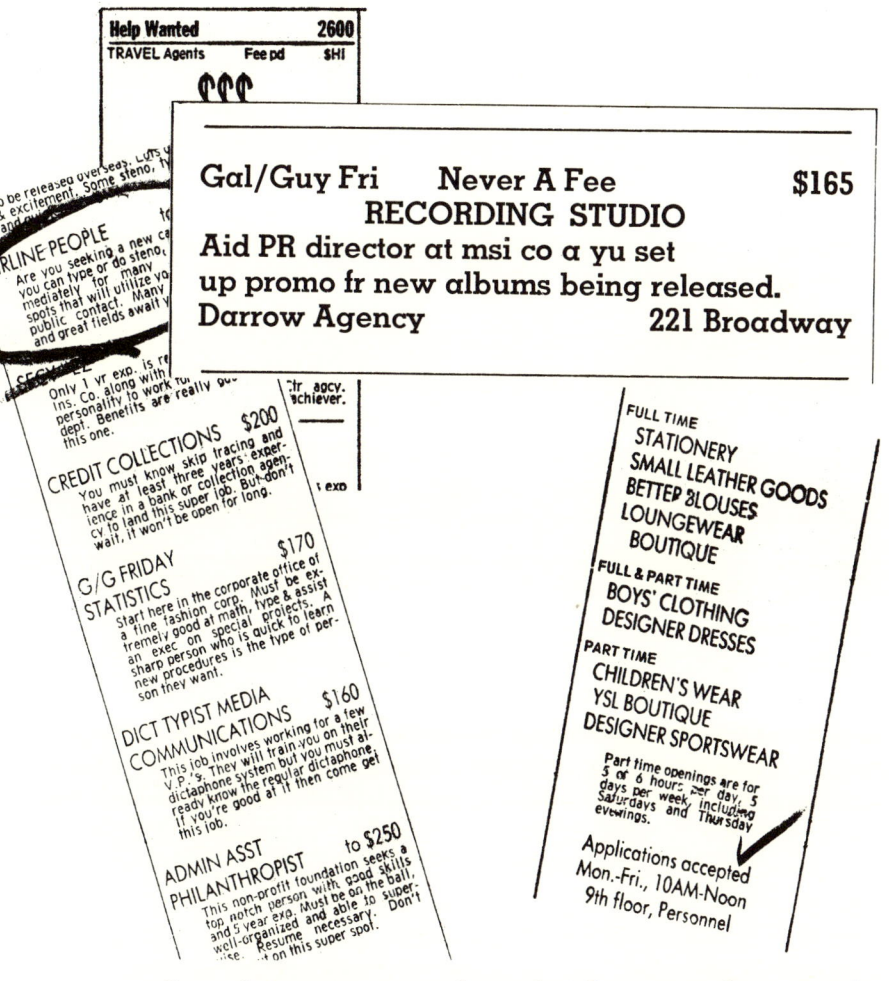

Sounds interesting doesn't it?—promotion, music company, records, possibly meet famous people. The salary of $165 a week will not make you rich, but it is a beginning.

Unfortunately that ad may not mean what it says. It could be a come-on ad to bring people to the agency; once you're there you are told that that particular job is filled but they have other positions, and are given an application form to fill out. Or the job could be available and when you go see about it, it's really just a clerical position. The point is not to get your hopes up over glamorous sounding jobs. If they turn out to be what they say they are, fine; the chances are they will not.

As you see in the above ad, you do not have to pay a fee to the employment agency—a fairly common practice these days. Now the burden is on the employer. That works to your advantage and disadvantage. Obviously it will save you money; on the other hand, when employers must pay a fee they are extremely cautious about who they hire—a mistake can be costly for them. Therefore, you as a potential employee will be subject to a more thorough scrutiny than if you were picking up the tab.

At the employment agency you will fill out an application (take a résumé to leave with the agency) and you will be interviewed by the interviewing agent. He or she may send you out on some job interviews immediately, or you might have to check back each week to see if anything is available. If certain jobs require a specific type of clothing—for example, women must wear skirts—the agency will tell you before sending you out.

Fill out all applications truthfully. You could get a job by lying, but if you're found out, it's quite likely you will be fired.

Don't misrepresent your skills on an application. For instance, one young woman answered the question "Can you type?" with a "Yes." "I figured any fool can type," she recalls. The next question was, "How many words per minute?" She put down 45 to 50. When she was given a typing test she actually typed

5 words per minute. "I was grateful I was at the agency and not with the employer," she remembers with embarrassment. "The interviewer asked whatever made me say I could type. I said I always typed my school papers. She explained that I could hunt and peck, or I could type what was in my own head because I was looking at the keys. After that I learned to say that I could type well enough to handle my own correspondence."

Some positions are advertised by the employer so you can eliminate one step and go directly to the place that is hiring. This is much less frustrating because you don't have to work through a third person. Unfortunately, however, in large cities the bulk of the positions advertised come through agencies.

Another approach is to register with the personnel departments of some large companies you think you might like to work for. Sometimes there will be immediate openings, other times they will put your application in their files and tell you they will call you if something comes up.

Whether or not you will get a job quickly is hard to determine. Much job hunting is a matter of luck—you happen to be around when your particular skills are needed. The point is not to get discouraged if you don't find something immediately. The competition is tough and you can not expect overnight success. Keep in mind that being rejected for a position is not a rejection of you as a person. It just may mean that someone else has more experience or a greater number of skills than you have.

On the other hand, if you are told by several employers that you need more skills than you now possess, you seriously ought to consider working at a less demanding job while taking courses to get some additional training.

Should an interviewer at an agency tell you to check in each week, don't be shy about following through. The agent's job is to find you work, and you're not bothering anyone by dropping in or making a phone call. It is the people who make themselves heard who get attention, so you needn't feel you're out-of-line by acting in your own best interests. Interviewers see a great many people and the only way they will remember you is if you keep in touch. That doesn't mean you should be a pest, but it does mean you have to speak up for yourself.

Eventually your persistence will pay off and you will find a job. It may not be the one you dreamed of, and the salary might be lower than you had in mind, but it is a beginning. Once you are self-supporting, you are truly an adult.

It would be nice if once you have a job everything would go along perfectly. It never happens that way. Life is filled with problems, and very often they are job-related. Sometimes they loom as insoluble. This is usually because problems can create panic, and panic tends to blot out the various choices that are usually available to you. Other times you might let things slide because the difficulty doesn't seem very important. You hope that it will go away or somehow resolve itself. The opposite usually occurs—the problem gets bigger and more unwieldy. So when difficulties occur remember two things: view your problems as calmly as possible; take action immediately.

The following are some problems that could arise in connection with your job:

THE BOSS DOES NOT LIKE YOU AND SHOWS IT

First make sure that it is not your imagination. Check it out with your coworkers—Do they perceive the hostility toward you? If they confirm your own perceptions, you may have to decide to quit, especially if the hostility is hurting your chances of advancing in the company. You can try to transfer to another section or department but other than that you don't have many options. When there is a clash of personalities it is often impossible to do much about it. Most often these dislikes of someone are totally irrational and have nothing to do with anything the person is doing. If everyone else likes you except this one individual, do not take it personally, but do take steps to alleviate an uncomfortable, and possibly damaging situation.

YOU ARE FIRED

Getting the sack can happen to anyone, but it is always an upsetting experience. You cannot help feeling that somehow you have failed, even though the firing may have occurred because the office or plant is cutting back on personnel and not because you are ineffective at your job. Just be aware that the feelings of rejection will pass and you will get another job— maybe even a better one. If you have been fired for incompetence or a poor attitude, do not make excuses for yourself. Face up to your own responsibility for being let go and decide what you can do about it. If you don't confront the reason for having been fired you'll only repeat the same mistakes in the next job.

YOU DO NOT GET ALONG WITH YOUR COWORKERS

If you do not get on with **any** of the people you work with, it very likely has something to do with your behavior and attitude. Try to be honest about this. Do you have difficulty with people off the job? If that is your pattern, you will have to do something to remedy it. On the other hand, it could be that this group of workers is an especially unpleasant collection of people, and if you really can't stand them then look for another job.

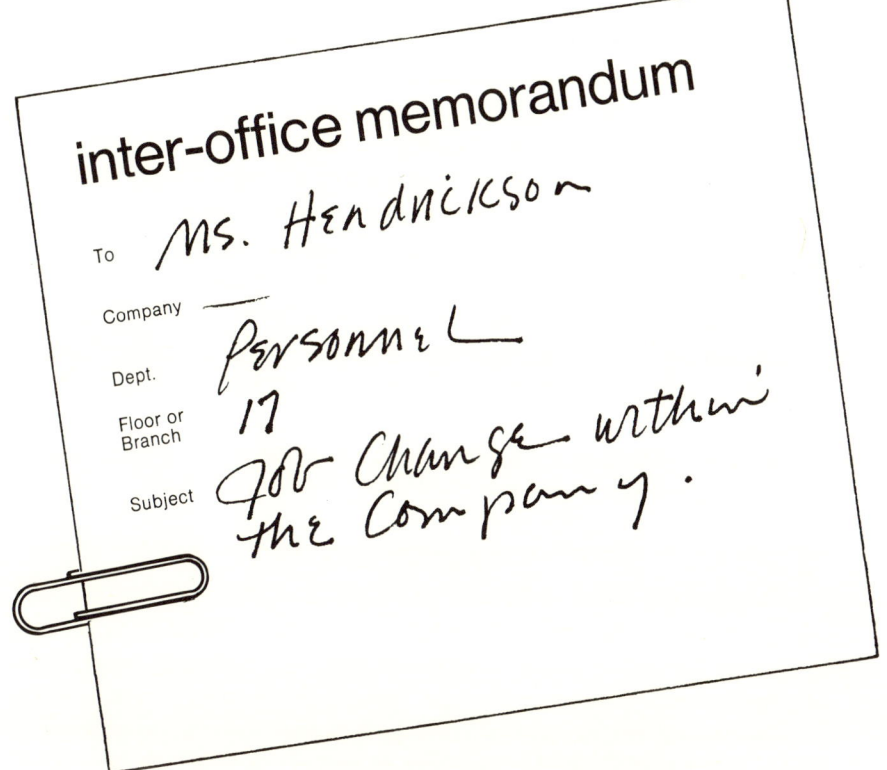

YOU HATE YOUR JOB BUT THE PAY AND BENEFITS ARE TERRIFIC

This is a common problem, and there are many middle-aged men and women who have glumly stuck it out in a hated job because they don't want to give up the money and the extras. You can make that choice, but bear in mind that working for years at something you dislike will affect you. It can make you bitter and unhappy, and you might wonder if the tradeoff is worth it. Our society encourages us to take the job that pays the most. Indeed you do want to make a good living, but sometimes it is to your advantage to earn less in order to enjoy your life more. Ideally, of course, you want to find the job you love with a fabulous salary and great benefits. It can happen, but there are times when you have to compromise. How you compromise is your choice.

QUITTING A JOB GRACEFULLY

If possible, do not leave one position until you have found another. Aside from the fact that you won't have a period of unemployment, it is to your advantage to look for a job while still working. You will not feel as desperate. And you are more impressive to personnel people when you are presently employed.

Since you might want a future reference from your employer, try to make the leave-taking as pleasant as possible. Give enough notice and if possible offer to train your replacement. Should you dislike your boss, do not use the last day to tell him or her off. Nothing will be accomplished and you'll lose a potential letter of recommendation.

MEDDLING

If you are very competent at your work, you may feel impelled to tell other people how to do their job. **Don't.** Stick to your own work unless, of course, someone asks for assistance. Too much help from you only serves to make the other person feel incompetent and resentful. On the other hand, what do you do when a coworker offers you too much help? At first it is tempting to let someone else take the responsibility off your shoulders but after awhile you begin to feel irritated, guilty, and inadequate. Do your job as well as you can and let others do theirs. That is why you were all hired.

YOU ARE BEING OVERWHELMED WITH EXCESSIVE WORK

Don't just sit there and grumble about it. You can explain to your employer that you were hired to do certain designated tasks and now you have been given many extras to do. You can either ask for a raise to cover the excessive work or you can request that the work load be lightened. Your request will probably be met. If not, you'll have to decide if it is worth staying under the circumstances.

ASKING FOR A RAISE

Most places give automatic raises every few years, but sometimes, when you are doing excellent work and you feel your salary isn't equal to your competence, you will want to ask for a raise. This is something you should do in a very straightforward way. Point out to your employer that you have a better-than-average work record and that you deserve a higher salary. The chances are, if you are a valuable employee, you will get your raise. However, in some companies there are fixed salaries and no possibility of getting an increase no matter how good you are. If you like the job a lot, you may decide that you'll do without more money.

In a situation where a raise is possible, and you know you have a great deal to offer your employer, you can threaten to leave unless you get more money. Just be sure you really mean what you're saying, and that you're not tossing out empty threats. If the raise is refused and you stay on after threatening to leave, you will have lost some measure of respect, and your boss won't take you seriously in the future.

Don't ask for a raise by telling your employer how hard your life is and how many debts you have. This is not his or her concern. You're entitled to a raise for doing good work, not because you have mismanaged your personal life.

YOU'RE CAUGHT DOING SOMETHING NOT QUITE HONEST SUCH AS MAKING LONG-DISTANCE CALLS ON THE COMPANY PHONE OR TAKING THINGS FROM THE STOCKROOM

If you are guilty admit it. Don't make phony excuses. Don't say you didn't know the rules. Tell your employer you are sorry and will not do it again, and stick to your promise.

These are only a few examples, but they can give you an idea of the kinds of things that could happen. No matter what occurs, take the time to think each problem through and to choose the solution that serves you best. Be as honest with yourself as you can in confronting your own responsibility in a situation. Do not ignore the problem—it will only get worse as time passes. It is your job and you might as well get as much satisfaction from it as you can.

Now that you are making money, what do you do with it? Why spend it of course. At least that's the answer you will get every time you open a newspaper or a magazine, or turn on your television or radio. The advertisements shout out to you to buy. Everything is a bargain you can't afford to miss. If you don't have the cash on hand, charge it, pay for it on the installment plan, dig into your savings, but do not deny yourself **anything!**

That is what you'll do if you pay attention to the media. If you listen to your own good sense, you'll have some second thoughts before rushing out to the department stores. There is no question that in the beginning most of you will need a great many things. Setting up housekeeping is unavoidable and expensive. Let's face it, it's no fun drinking your morning orange juice from your toothbrush glass, or spending your nights curled up in a sleeping bag.

Those of you moving into a roommate's furnished apartment will not face this problem (although you'll still be confronted with saving and spending decisions). If you can take furniture and supplies from your parents' home you'll also avoid a large outlay of money.

The rest of you will have to do a little spending. Just take it slowly. You want to avoid piling up an enormous debt. You can't imagine how easy it is to get into that predicament if you're not careful. Your first task is to decide what you **need.** Think only of essentials. Your second step is to determine what you can **afford** to have now. When you know what you need and what you can afford, you can then come to grips with the best way to pay for things. There is a lot to be said for paying cash for all purchases: you don't become involved with monthly payments; the item is immediately yours; you pay less by avoiding the monthly interest you must pay for credit.

Regrettably, cash is not always on hand. If you must have a bed to sleep in, or clothes to put on your back, you will have to resort to borrowing, or to charging now and paying later. There is one advantage to charge account buying—you build up a sound credit rating. In other words, if you pay your bills in full at the end of the month, or if you scrupulously send in the monthly installments toward the total amount, you will go on record as being a good financial risk. Should you ever need to borrow money, your chances of getting a loan will be vastly superior to those of the person who has always paid cash at the time of purchase. Sounds crazy, doesn't it? It is absolutely true. The individual who has paid cash through the years may find it impossible to get a mortgage loan on a house he or she wants to buy. The reason—no credit rating.

With all that said, you should still be cautious about purchasing on credit. It can get out of hand. And

before you know it you're still paying off purchases you've long stopped using. What could be more depressing than paying monthly installments on a television set that no longer functions?

The other disadvantage of buying on time is that you pay more for the item than if you had purchased it outright. If you charge something on May 1, and pay for it on June 1, you won't have to pay interest. However, some banks are beginning to charge a fee to credit-card users who pay their bills in full each month. The bank only makes money on the customer who is paying the interest rates. The interest rate doesn't look like much when tacked onto each installment, but when you add it all up, the additional amount could be as high as $100, depending on the price of the item purchased. It may be worth your while to pay the extra money. But you owe it to yourself to weigh the pros and cons before you commit yourself to months, and sometimes years, of installment payments.

YOUR SECONDHAND CAR

If you don't know about automobiles, have someone who is knowledgeable check it out before you buy it. Ask the following questions:

Is the car worth the price?

Does it need any major repairs? Make sure you can afford them if it does.

Are the tires in good condition? A car with worn tires is unsafe, and if you cannot afford new ones, then find a car for which you won't have to make the investment.

Will you get adequate mileage per gallon of gasoline? That is very important with the price of gasoline constantly going up.

Is this a car that is liable to cause you trouble in the future? You don't want to have to plunk down several hundred dollars in six months.

As an automobile owner, you should:

Learn to do minor repairs yourself in order to save money and so you will not be totally dependent upon others.

Keep the car in good condition so that it operates safely and efficiently.

Always use the seat belts even though they are a bore. They do save lives.

Drive within the speed limit. You save gasoline, and you may even save your life.

MAJOR TYPES OF AUTOMOBILE INSURANCE COVERAGE

CODE	MEANING	COVERAGE
A	Bodily injury liability	Anybody you hurt will be taken care of.
B	Property damage liability	Any car you crash into will be repaired.
C	Medical payments	Your passengers will be treated.
D	Comprehensive	Your car's non-crash damage will be repaired.
E	Fire, wind, theft	Your stolen car will be replaced.
G	Deductible collision	Within preset limits, your car will be repaired.
H	Emergency road service	Your tow charge will be paid.
U	Uninsured motorist	Your damages will be repaired even if an uninsured driver hits you.

Borrowing money is another way of paying for things, but again it's something to think about first. Should you borrow from parents, friends, or the bank?

Parents are often a good source of loans, although not always. It depends on your relationship. Some parents use the fact that you have to borrow as a way of putting you down, while others will understand the dilemma and will be helpful. The loan can be set up in a couple of ways. You can pay the same amount of interest as a bank would charge. Your parents may be content to forgo the interest. You can repay a lump sum at a given time. You can pay monthly installments.

If you don't get along with your parents and borrowing from them will put you in an unequal position with them, try to find another source. However, if you are desperate, and they are the only ones with money, you will have to work something out. If you make the arrangement as businesslike as possible, you won't feel quite so uncomfortable.

Borrowing from friends can also present problems. In a moment of largesse a friend may say, "Take as long as you want to repay me." The next month he or she is asking how long before you can return the money. Many a friendship has been ruined by borrowing and lending money. If you value the friendship, look elsewhere.

Banks will often lend money based on the savings you have in your account. This is called a passbook loan. If you have $1000 in your account, and you don't want to spend it, the bank will lend you $1000 and freeze your account until the loan is repaid. The bank charges you a small interest rate on the borrowed money, while your banked money is earning dividends, so the loan costs you very little. You can take as long as two years, making small monthly payments, to repay the money. Look into other possible loans at your local bank. Borrowing from a bank is very good for your credit rating.

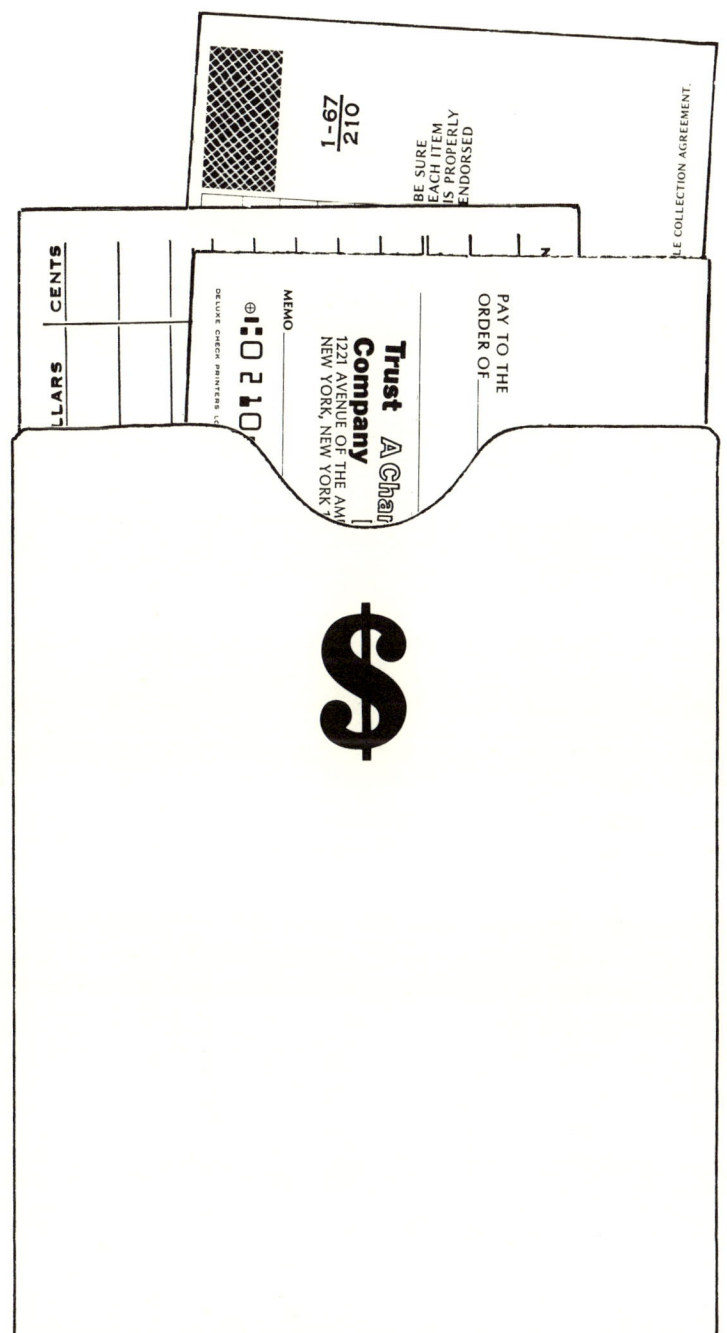

SAMPLE MONTHLY BUDGET FOR $165 A WEEK

	RENT	FOOD	UTILITIES	PHONE	CLOTHES	SAVINGS	ENTERTAINMENT	DEBTS	MISC.
Totals:	$170	$80	$15	$12	$50	$20	$80	$50	$83
1st week	42.50	15	3.75	3	0	5	20	12.50	10
2nd week	42.50	20	3.75	3	25	5	10	12.50	25
3rd week	42.50	35	3.75	3	100	5	0	12.50	19
4th week	42.50	25	3.75	3	0	5	18	12.50	20

As you can see, for this month less was spent on entertainment and more was spent on food than the allotted amount on the budget. It all evens out because the extra money on entertainment can be applied to food. The budget went over on clothes allowance, so next month will allocate less for clothes. Miscellaneous is left with a few dollars to apply to next month's miscellaneous.

Some of you will want to set up your budget differently. You may wish to make more items rather than lumping them under miscellaneous, debts, and entertainment. You could include transportation, books and records, gifts, medical, etc. You will also allot different amounts for different activities, depending on your lifestyle. If you have an automobile, don't forget to include a section on automobile maintenance.

In addition to thinking about spending, give some thought to how you will save. A good rule to follow—no matter how small the paycheck—is to put some portion of your earnings into the savings bank each week. It doesn't have to be a large sum—it could be as little as $5.00—but you should bank something. Once you start saving, make it an action you do automatically; and don't withdraw any of the money, even in an emergency. View it as money you don't have. Forget about it and let it continue to earn interest. Naturally there will come a time when you will want to use it for something special, but if you have allowed it to accumulate for several years, you'll really have some savings to work with.

Budgeting is something else to consider. Try to apportion your salary over the week so you're not spending everything on entertainment and clothes with little left over for rent and utilities. You could make a chart with headings such as: rent, food, utilities, phone, clothes, savings, entertainment, debt payments, miscellaneous.

Debt payments not only include paying back a loan, but indicates payments you are making on a doctor's or dentist's bill or an item you have purchased that is not clothing. Entertainment covers movies, sports events, restaurants, parties at home, and any other activities that are just for fun. Miscellaneous items are all the extras—shoe repair, drug store products, haircuts, stationery, a book or record you might want.

In filling out your chart, enter the constant expenses first—rent, phone, utilities, savings, and debt payments. Then figure out how much money is left over and the best way to divide it for your other needs. If you find the budget doesn't work exactly as you've set it up, you may have to readjust it. You will probably need about a month of practice to design a budget that reflects your lifestyle.

Of course some items are flexible. For example, you may budget $25 a week for clothes; three weeks could go by and you spend nothing on clothing. The fourth week you spend $100. That fits right into your budget. Should you spend $125, you can deny yourself a purchase the following week. The same rule applies to entertainment.

Not everyone needs or wants a formal budget. Some people can sort things out in their head, while others prefer to stay loose about money. Some people set up a budget for a few months in order to establish spending habits, and then do away with the weekly written entries. A budget doesn't have to be set up on a weekly basis only. You could have a biweekly or monthly budget instead.

Whatever you decide, your main concern should be to know where your money goes, and to have some control over it. It's a horrible feeling to look in your wallet at the end of the day and to think, panic-struck, "I had $50 this morning. Where did it go?" That will happen to you occasionally, but the less frequently the better.

7
Food and you

Most of you have probably taken food for granted all your life. What has gone into your stomach has been purchased, prepared, and set before you by your parents. Your only job has been to eat it.

Now you must do the planning, buying, and cooking of whatever you consume. It is not a difficult job, but it does require some thought and knowledge. All of you should cook—men and women. Too often, rather than learning to feed themselves properly, men will get married so they can have a built-in cook and housekeeper. That's a poor excuse for taking a lifetime partner. Learn to cook for yourself, and marry for more solid reasons.

Cooking is fun. It is creative and can give pleasure to others as well as to yourself. Cooking is only dreary when you feel inadequate in the kitchen. The truth is, anyone who can read a recipe can be a more than adequate cook.

Start by finding a good cookbook—one that gives very clear directions. The **Joy of Cooking** by Irma S. Rombauer and Marion Rombauer Becker is one of the best. It answers all sorts of food questions and the recipes range from very simple to gourmet. For vegetarians, **The Vegetarian Epicure** by Anna Thomas is a must. There is not a bad recipe in the whole book. Indeed, the quality is so high that a sample of a few dishes might convert the most dedicated meat eater. **Good Cheap Food** by Miriam Ungerer is another terrific cookbook, especially for the hard-pressed budget. All the above can be purchased in paperback.

In addition to your cookbook, ask your parents for recipes for some of your favorite dishes. A cookbook and a few recipes will equip you for several years of good eating. If you really get involved in cooking, you will probably start clipping recipes from newspapers and magazines, and you will become interested in more specialized cookbooks.

Planning meals in advance is a great time and money saver. If you know what you will cook for a week, or even for several days, you can spend one day at the supermarket a week, and you're through—except for the occasional quart of milk or loaf of bread. Pay attention to sales and buy accordingly. Newspapers generally print ads for sale items on a certain day of the week so you know what is reduced even before you go shopping. If chicken and pot roast are on sale, include them in your menu for the week. Do the same with fruits and vegetables and desserts.

When planning meals, try to balance them. That means you should include a variety of vitamins and minerals rather than just a few—a meal that consists of hamburger and french fries is unbalanced; add a green vegetable and a piece of fruit and it is balanced.

As you probably know, all meals should contain some protein, which you can get from meat, fish, cheese, eggs, a combination of beans and rice, lentils, yogurt, and milk. Yogurt and milk aren't as high in protein as the other products, but they are excellent supplements. Yogurt in particular is very healthful—great for the digestion—and you should try to become a yogurt fancier.

Dark green and yellow vegetables are necessary for their high vitamin A and mineral content. If possible, have them at lunch and supper. Salads are terrific, especially if you use romaine lettuce or watercress. They are much higher in vitamins than iceberg lettuce. Raw spinach also makes a good salad. In fact, vegetables don't always have to be cooked. Raw mushrooms, cauliflower, stringbeans, and broccoli are delicious in salads, and so is raw zucchini. A vegetable salad with some hardboiled eggs, cheese, ham, or chicken cut into it can make a perfect summer meal—all you need is a loaf of good bread on the side.

Foods that have vitamin C are also extremely important. That is a vitamin the body doesn't store, so you have to replenish it daily. A glass of orange juice each morning is a good source, as is half a grapefruit (studies have shown that frozen orange juice is even higher in vitamin C than fresh, so feel free to stock up on a few cans on sale days). Tomatoes, cranberries, and canteloupe are other fruits high in vitamin C.

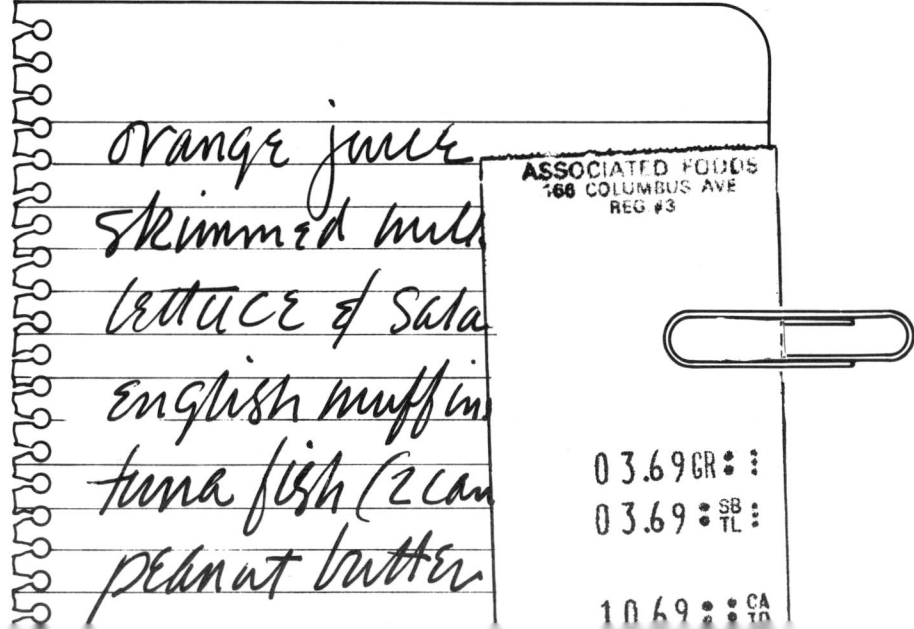

Try to kick the junk-food habit. Those items are expensive and lacking in nutrition. They simply fill you up so you're not hungry for more valuable foods. Once you become accustomed to eating nourishing meals, you'll be surprised to discover that the junk variety is almost unappealing. Besides, many of the snack foods have so many chemical additives that you really don't know what you're putting into your stomach.

Which brings up another important point—be a label reader. All packaged and canned foods list their ingredients, and it's the smart consumer who reads before buying. You might decide that you prefer the food with less additives to the ones with a long column of unpronounceable chemical names. Since one never knows which chemical will be proclaimed dangerous by the FDA, Food and Drug Administration, better to steer clear of them as much as possible.

You should also know that frozen and packaged goods are always more expensive than food you prepare yourself. Sometimes, when you are in a hurry, these foods are very convenient, but if you have time, do your own cooking.

Do use the freezer, however, for your own concoctions. For example, if you make a spaghetti sauce and use part of it, you can freeze the remainder for a future meal. Don't leave things too long in the freezer, though. A month is just about long enough for most foods.

Speaking of spaghetti sauce, knowing a delicious and easy recipe for a sauce, or for chili con carne, can solve some company menus. Almost everybody loves spaghetti and meat sauce, and chili, so have one on hand when you don't feel like being too fancy.

The following is a spaghetti sauce you can make at the last minute (most sauces have to cook for several hours) and it tastes even better the second day. If you make it without meat, it can be used for lasagna or any other Italian dish requiring a tomato sauce. Feel free to adjust the seasonings to suit your taste.

SPAGHETTI AND MEAT SAUCE
about 4 servings

½ onion diced
2 cloves of garlic
2 Tablespoons (30 ml) olive oil
½ pound lean ground chuck or round (227 g)
1 29 ounce can (822g.) of tomato puree
½ teaspoon (2.5 ml) dried basil
½ teaspoon (2.5 ml) dried oregano
½ teaspoon (2.5 ml) dried rosemary
1 bay leaf
1 teaspoon (5 ml) sugar
1 teaspoon (5 ml) salt

Put the garlic through a garlic press, and sauté it and the onion in the heated oil in a large frying pan. When the onion is soft, add the meat and sauté until brown. Turn the flame down low and add the other ingredients. Cover and simmer over a very low flame for half an hour to an hour. Stir it from time to time so it doesn't stick.

Boil a package of extra-thin spaghetti, following the directions on the box. Put the drained spaghetti in the center of individual plates, and pour some sauce over each portion.

Serve with freshly grated parmesan cheese, a green salad with Italian dressing, and french bread and butter.

The **Joy of Cooking** recipe for chili is excellent and also goes well with bread and salad. Make it one or two days ahead because it will be thicker.

So you see, putting a meal on the table needn't be an arduous or expensive task. As you become more skillful, you might want to try more complicated recipes, even going as far as baking some bread—the **James Beard Bread Book** is good. You can find bread recipes in the cookbooks already mentioned in this chapter. For now, take it slow and learn to make a few good basic meals.

Eating is one of the joys of life and so, believe it or not, is cooking.

TIPPING

In big cities, tipping ranges from ten to twenty-five percent of the total bill.

In a restaurant where you sit at a counter, a ten-percent tip is sufficient.

A fifteen-percent tip is expected if you are served at a table.

The fancier the restaurant, the larger is the tip that you are expected to leave.

When you are served by two or three waiters or waitresses, a tip of twenty-five percent is sufficient to cover all of them.

If you linger over a meal for a long time, it is polite to leave a larger tip. After all, your long stay has cost the waiter or waitress the tip that would have been left by another patron.

It is all right not to tip a sullen or rude waiter or waitress.

A LARGE PARTY FOR LITTLE MONEY

You can have a party for as many as fifty people and figure on spending about a dollar a person; the trick is to serve only wine, cheese, and raw vegetables.

A half gallon (1.89 liters) of wine can be purchased for as little as $2.00. Figure on seven half-gallon bottles. You can return the unopened bottles to the liquor store.

A wheel of brie, a large piece of Jarlsberg and another large piece of Vermont cheddar (or any other cheese you prefer) is all the cheese you need.

Four loaves of bread—French, rye, pumpernickel—and two boxes of sesame crackers will be ample and delicious with the cheese. Cut the bread into halves or quarters. Leftover bread can be frozen.

Two bunches of broccoli, blanched and cut into flowerettes (you blanch by putting the vegetables into boiling water and immediately draining them, making them greener and more tender), two bunches of carrots, scrubbed and cut into small slices lengthwise, two pounds of string beans, blanched and cut in half if they are very long, and two bunches of radishes, washed and trimmed, can be arranged on a large tray with a dish of your favorite dip in the middle. (Feel free to add any other vegetables you like, such as celery, cauliflower and mushrooms.)

If avocados are in season and fairly reasonable, make a large bowl of guacamole and surround it with taco or tortilla chips.

You will have more than enough food, and if the people are nice it should be a great party.

HIGH CALORIE FOODS
If you want to lose weight, keep away!

- avocado
- bacon (and foods cooked with bacon fat)
- baked or dried beans
- cake
- candy
- chocolate
- coconut
- cookies
- corn
- cream (sweet or sour)
- doughnuts
- fat meat
- French dressing
- fried foods
- fruit (dried or canned in syrup)
- gefilte fish
- gravy
- honey
- ice cream
- jams, jellies, or preserves
- luncheon meats
- macaroni
- malted milk
- mayonnaise
- milk shakes
- muffins
- nuts
- olives
- pancakes and waffles
- pastry
- peanut butter
- peas (dried, such as black-eyed)
- pie
- pizza
- popcorn
- pork
- potato chips
- pretzels
- puddings
- rolls
- spaghetti
- soda (ginger ale, cola drinks, etc.)
- sugar
- syrups

LOW CALORIE FOODS
These are good for you—fat or thin!

- apples
- apricots
- asparagus
- bean sprouts
- beef (lean)
- bouillon
- cabbage
- cantaloupe
- carrots
- cauliflower
- celery
- chicken
- clams
- coffee (no milk or sugar)
- cottage cheese
- cucumbers
- fish
- grapefruit
- lemon juice
- lettuce
- lime juice
- lobster
- mushrooms
- mustard
- oranges
- parsley
- pears
- peppers (red and green)
- pickles
- pimentos
- radishes
- sauces (such as Worcestershire and Tabasco)
- sauerkraut
- scallions
- seasonings (most herbs and spices)
- soda (plain)
- spinach
- strawberries
- string beans (French style)
- summer squash
- tangerines
- tea (no milk or sugar)
- tomatoes
- veal

IF ALL ELSE FAILS

In spite of the best advice in the world, many single people simply will not cook properly for themselves mainly because it seems like a lot of trouble for someone who is going to be eating alone. One single woman living in New York City has found a way around this. She invites guests for dinner at least two nights a week. The meal is nothing fancy, just meat, vegetables, and a starch. However, having guests (they help pay for groceries) guarantees that she eats well at least two nights each week.

FOOD BUYING TIPS

Buy perishable goods in small amounts. These are items such as vegetables, dairy products, and cereals.

Buy small sizes of food items you don't use regularly. Although small sizes are often more expensive, you will not have leftovers that might spoil. Also, you will not deny yourself eating something you like simply because you know you won't eat all of it.

Check spoilage dates (sometimes labeled "last date of sale") on dairy products, baked goods, and some meats.

Read the newspaper and clip coupons for sale items.

Buy large sizes of laundry items when they are on sale.

CHOOSING A DOCTOR

Because you are young, your chances of becoming seriously ill are quite slim. However, there will be occasions when you will want to see a doctor. If you're away from your hometown, you won't be able to count on the tried-and-true family physician.

If you are in a city that has a good health center (some towns have a woman's health center as well) you can avail yourself of its services. Hospitals with well established clinics are also good sources of medical care. But those of you who want to have your own doctor should take some time to look for someone qualified and personable.

Most people put off choosing a doctor until they are sick. Then they frantically phone friends and hospitals in an effort to find someone to treat them. That's the wrong way to choose a physician. Make your selection when you're feeling well—when it's time for your yearly checkup. There are several ways to go about this: You can get a referral from a friend. You can call a medical school and ask for a physician on their staff (they will give you several names of their younger physicians). You can call the county medical society and ask for some names. If there is a woman's group in the community, women can call it and ask for referrals.

While men, and many women, will want an internist as the primary-care physician, some women may opt for an obstetrician-gynecologist. Most ob/gyns realize that some women have no other doctor than themselves, and they will do a more thorough examination than the routine pelvic. They can also act as a referral physician, and will put you in touch with specialists when you need them. Since the majority of women visit their gynecologists more often than their internists (women should go for yearly pap-smear tests and breast examinations) it sometimes makes sense to use the gynecologist as the primary-care doctor.

When you have received a few names from one of the above sources, you can begin checking their qualifications. The best way is to call a doctor's office and ask the nurse some of the following questions:

Is the physician board certified? That means he or she has had an approved residency and has passed the written board examinations. Passing the oral exams makes the doctor board qualified, but being board certified means the physician will soon be taking the orals, and that's okay for your purposes.

Where was the physician trained? If the doctor graduated from a good medical school, that means the training was of higher calibre.

With which hospital is the doctor affiliated? You want a physician who is connected with one of the better hospitals—preferably a teaching hospital—and one that is convenient to you. Avoid doctors who have no hospital affiliation, even if they are fine physicians. If there is an emergency, or if you need surgery, you want to be sure of hospital care with the best possible facilities. You also want to be sure you can get there quickly.

You can ask the doctor's sex, but you should not be guided by that. You are looking for a well-qualified physician with whom you can feel comfortable. If you can only be at ease with a woman, or you only trust a man, and you can find someone good of the proper gender, fine. If not, keep an open mind.

Will there be a long office wait for your appointment? If so, why? If the wait is because the doctor spends a long time with each patient, that's all right. You know you won't be given short shrift. If the long wait is because the physician tries to see ten patients in one hour, that's not all right. You don't want to feel like a body on an assembly line.

Feel free to ask any other questions that concern you.

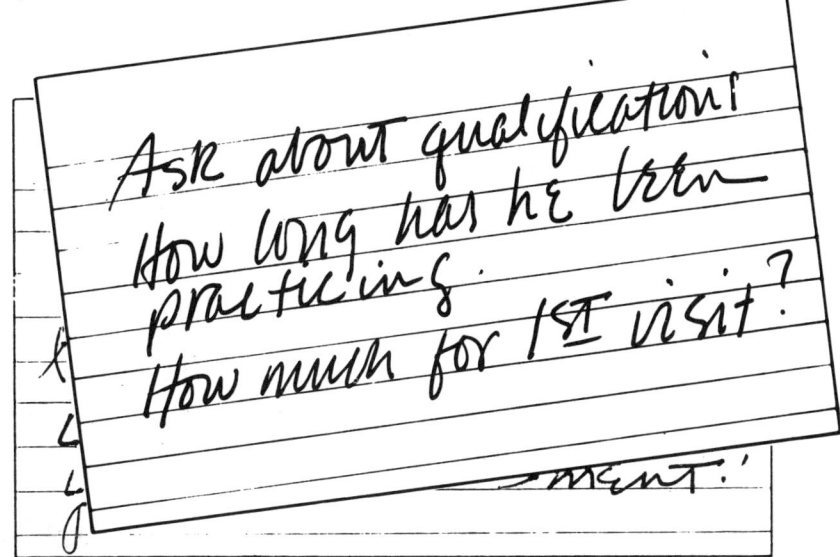

Your first appointment with your new doctor should be thought of as an interview as well as an examination. You want to find out if this is the person for you. It is a good idea to write down questions you want answered about any symptoms you might have before going to the office. If the doctor shuttles you out, and doesn't deal with your questions, you know you're not getting proper care. The doctor should also take a complete history on you—previous illnesses, any family diseases, any chronic problems—as well as getting to know a little of your lifestyle and your life circumstances.

Most important: Is the doctor willing to explain your symptoms? Will he or she reveal the reason for medication, offer you alternative medication, list side effects of medication being prescribed? Are you allowed to be part of the decision-making process? In short, does the physician treat you with consideration and respect?

If a doctor does not answer your questions, and does not give you an adequate examination, even though you have demanded your needs be met, you have a perfect right to withhold payment for your visit. Send a letter of explanation, pointing out the things you had asked for that were not done. Tell the physician that since you didn't get complete service, you will not pay the fee.

In response, the doctor could do one of the following: invite you back for a more thorough examination (pretty unlikely); forget about it since it's a small amount; turn it over to a collection agency, which can hound you but can't do much else (it might hurt your credit rating if you have a great many other unpaid bills but if you're up-to-date, it shouldn't have much effect—check with a lawyer if you're concerned); turn it over to a lawyer who might send you an intimidating letter or two. It is unlikely that you'll be taken to court over a relatively small sum.

```
         DAVID M. FRIEDMAN, O.D., F.A.A.O.
   36 EAST 36TH STREET
   NEW YORK, N. Y. 10016        11 OLD ORCHARD RD.
   212 MURRAY HILL 4-0994      NEW ROCHELLE, N. Y. 10804
                                914 NEW ROCHELLE 6-2006
```

FOR *Judie Mills* _____ DATE

℞		SPHERICAL	CYLINDRICAL	AXIS
DV	O. D.	−2.50	−1.00	165
	O. S.			
ADD	O. D.			
	O. S.			

REMARKS _____

```
            H. PHARMACEUTICALS INC.
         62 LEXINGTON AVE., NEW YORK, N.Y. 10021
               Phone RE 7-1230
 314454L        11-7-75
Take 1 capsule 3 times
a day when needed.
                           Dr Poll
```

This does not mean you should withhold a fee if your physician doesn't immediately cure your illness. Doctors are not magicians. But you can expect to be taken seriously, and to be listened to. The doctor should make every effort to cure your symptoms, and if he or she can't, you should be referred to another physician. If you say you have pain and the doctor can't find the cause, it is not acceptable to be told that there is nothing wrong with you and you are in pain because you are neurotic (women are told this more often than men). You are in pain because there is something wrong with you, and if that doctor can't diagnose it, get yourself to someone else.

If you are not satisfied with one physician, you should always feel free to change. You don't owe any doctor a loyalty. Don't rationalize by saying your present physician knows your history so you should stick with him or her. Your records from your first doctor can be sent to your second doctor. Unfortunately, you have no legal right to copies of your records, which means your new physician will have to request them. That holds true if you move to another city or state. Some states are beginning to introduce legislation allowing patients to have copies of doctor and hospital records, and some hospitals and doctors will, even now, give you copies, but at this time you have no legal claim on all the medical facts pertaining to your own body.

Once you have chosen a doctor, you will probably go for periodic checkups, or for minor symptoms, and that will be it. There could come a time, however, when you will have something more serious, and the physician will recommend surgery. Should that happen, it is in your best interest to seek another opinion, especially if major surgery is prescribed. Your goal is not to find a doctor who will assure you there is nothing wrong with you, but to get some assurance that surgery is actually necessary. If the consultant disagrees with your physician, you might have to seek a third opinion. This is not a recommendation to run from doctor to doctor, but you should feel convinced that all the knowables indicate you need surgery before deciding to go through with an operation. Don't worry that your doctor will feel insulted if you want to talk to someone else. It's your body you are dealing with, not the doctor's—a good point to remember at all times.

CHOOSING A DENTIST

A good many of you have been brought up to view the dentist as someone you go to when you have a toothache. Regular dental checkups have not been a part of your life As an adult you have the opportunity to change that pattern and you should.

There are several important reasons why regular dental checkups are necessary: you prevent the occurrence of toothaches by catching cavities when they are very small, and having them filled; your gums are checked for any diseases—should there be a problem they are treated before they can adversely affect your teeth; you'll probably never have to wear false teeth; you'll save a great deal of money in the long run because it's cheaper to go to the dentist once or twice a year for your entire life, than it is to have major dental work done when your teeth start to hurt and go rotten.

So don't wait until the only solution for an aching tooth is to pull it. Locate a dentist and make yearly checkups a part of your normal routine.

You can find a dentist through friends, through your family doctor, at a college of dentistry, or at a hospital that offers dental service. If the dentist is highly recommended, the chances are he or she is a competent practitioner. However, you want to be sure that this is the person for you, so you can check out a few things on your first visit:

Are the office and reception room clean and neat? Sloppy surroundings could indicate slipshod work habits.

Is the dentist on time for the appointment? Unless there's an emergency you shouldn't be kept waiting beyond fifteen or twenty minutes.

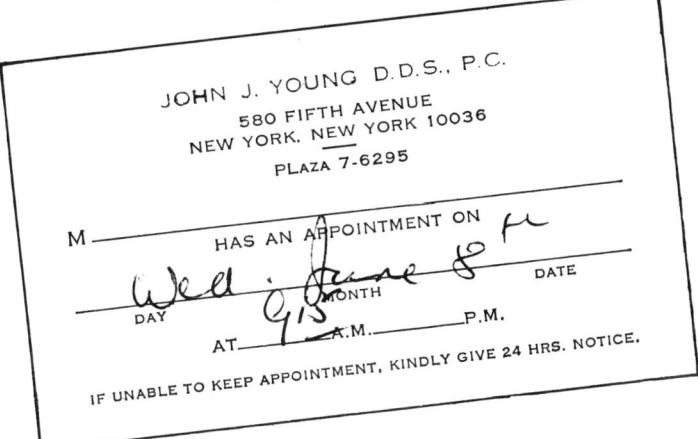

Is the staff pleasant? A dentist who cares about the patients will demand that his or her staff be kind and courteous to them.

Does the dentist take down your medical, as well as your dental, history? It is essential that he or she ask you about medications you are taking, or have taken, and if you have any allergies to pain-relieving drugs.

Feel free to ask some questions of your own.

Is the dentist available to treat you in an emergency? Is there another dentist you can call when your dentist is away?

Are payments accepted from Blue Cross or other dental plan insurers? If you don't have the insurance then this question is irrelevant for you.

If you are very sensitive to pain, ask if anesthesia is used, even for minimal work. Does the dentist have the latest equipment for drilling that is fast and almost painless? Having the latest and best equipment is not a must for a good dentist, but it's a real plus for the nervous patient who has a low pain threshold.

Does the dentist seem sympathetic and understanding when you speak of your nervousness? If not, find someone else.

How does the dentist feel about extracting teeth? A very important question—you want someone who believes in saving teeth, and only pulls as a last resort.

Does the dentist do periodic x-rays of your teeth. That is a must. X-rays are the only precise method for diagnosing dental problems. Naturally you don't want excessive x-rays because you don't want unnecessary exposure to radiation, but you do want them done periodically, depending on the condition of your teeth and gums.

Does the dentist provide a lead apron for young

women when they are having x-rays? Another must. The apron protects the reproductive organs from radiation fallout.

What are the fees? It's a good idea to have this discussion early on. The dentist can explain to you the cost of x-rays, why one cavity is more expensive to fill than another, and any other questions pertaining to payment.

A dentist should be receptive to all your queries. You have a right to ask about the care you're getting, especially if it's something that seems unusual to you. Should an expensive series of treatments be recommended, and you are uneasy about it, tell your dentist you want a second opinion. The dentist ought to be amenable to the idea, and should allow the consulting dentist to view your x-rays.

Occasionally a dentist detects a condition in your mouth that would be best treated by a specialist, and you are referred to one. Again, you have a right to ask details: What is the problem? What kind of treatment will you get? How expensive will it be? How long will it take?

Don't put off any necessary work because of the expense—that's being penny wise and pound foolish, since your teeth can only get worse. Most dentists will let you work out a payment plan that you can afford.

Sometimes two specialists will have vastly different fees simply because of the neighborhood in which they practice. An orthodontist in a fancy neighborhood could charge as much as $2,500 for braces (this is not to imply you'll need braces, but if you do, it is never too late to straighten crooked teeth), while an equally good one in a less fashionable area might charge as little as $800. Ask your dentist about this when a specialist is necessary.

There is always a chance—although a very slight one—of a dispute over a fee, and if you can't resolve it with your dentist, you can contact the local dental society. It will refer your dispute to its Mediation or Patient Relations Committee where your case will be investigated. When the matter involves a prepaid program under a dental insurance policy, your case will be referred to the Peer Review Committee.

Never be afraid to change dentists. After several visits you may decide you really don't feel comfortable with this individual, or you don't quite trust his or her approach to dentistry. Even if this person has been touted as highly skilled, you have to abide by your own feelings. There are other dentists equally competent, and there's no need to stay with someone with whom you are not happy.

CHOOSING A PSYCHIATRIST, PSYCHOANALYST, PSYCHOTHERAPIST

Everyone gets depressed, anxious, and fearful occasionally, but there are times when the emotions seem overwhelming and intractable. Nothing you do makes you feel better, and you fervently wish that you could find a way to alleviate these oppressive feelings that are getting in the way of a productive lifestyle.

Some of you may decide that your problems are so out of hand that you would like some help from a psychoanalyst or psychotherapist. But how do you find someone competent and reputable? It isn't easy. Unlike doctors and dentists, it is extremely hard to judge the quality of a psychotherapist or psychoanalyst. Emotional changes are not as clearcut as physical changes so it is difficult to determine whether or not someone is helping you. With all that said, if you use your own instincts and judgment in assessing the person you choose, and if that person seems to be honest, consistent, and totally trustworthy, the chances are you will get some help. A relationship with an analyst or therapist is much like any other relationship, and ultimately only you can decide if it is right for you.

Here are a few guidelines for choosing a therapist or analyst. First of all, don't get too bogged down in terminology. Whether an individual is a psychoanalyst, psychiatrist, or psychotherapist is not as important as how they behave with you. Many of these people function in the same way regardless of title, and the names only indicate the kind of training they have completed. For the record, however, a psychiatrist is a medical doctor who has specialized in the field of psychiatry. A psychoanalyst has graduated from one of the several analytic schools in the country and has been trained to help people change in very basic ways rather than to simply work out current problems, although they do deal with current problems. Some psychiatrists are psychoanalysts and some Ph.D.s in psychology have also gone to analytic school and qualify as analysts. Psychotherapist is a general term applied to anyone who isn't trained at an analytic school. Therefore a Ph.D. in psychology can be a therapist and so can a person with a Masters Degree in Social Work. Therapists usually deal with problems of the moment, although many actually are concerned with more overall changes.

All of the above, except for the Master of Social Work (they are called psychiatric social workers) can be listed as doctors on your income tax forms, allowing you a deduction for medical expenses. Of course only the M.D.s are actually medical people, and only they can prescribe drugs if needed. However, M.D.s are no more capable than Ph.D.s or M.S.W.s, (sometimes they are even less capable) so don't reject someone just because there's no M.D. after the name.

In finding someone to help you with your problems (to simplify things I'll refer to them all as analysts from here on), you can do the following: call the psychiatric division of your local hospital; call Jewish, Catholic, or

Protestant agencies; if there is a mental health center in your city, call and ask for referrals; if you have a friend who seems to have made some positive changes while going to an analyst, ask for the name of the analyst; women's organizations can usually give you a referral (men as well as women); churches and synagogues are also good sources. Of late, many ministers and rabbis have gone back to school to get some special training in psychology so they can be of help to their congregation when there are emotional problems to be confronted. Analytic schools can give you names of their graduates, or they can refer you to their clinic where you are helped by well-supervised very advanced students.

Many hospitals and agencies have clinics. If you qualify you can see someone for a minimal fee. The only problem with clinics is that you can not always choose the person who will be your analyst. However, if you dislike the assigned analyst they will usually make a change. Another drawback is that there is a turnover in clinics—students graduate or the analysts cannot devote time to the clinic because of the demands in their private practice. You may become comfortable with one person only to have him or her leave, and you must start over with someone else. That doesn't always happen, but it is a possibility you should inquire about if you are looking into agencies or hospital clinics.

Once you have gotten a few names you can begin your interviews. Do not go to the first person you see, unless you like that person a lot. Take time deciding who you feel comfortable and trusting with. It will cost you the analyst's hourly fee, and you may not want to pay two or three fees in order to make a decision, but you will save money in the long run. If you get started with someone you do not really like and respect, you will ultimately want to leave that individual and money and time will have been wasted.

- Dr. Marvin William
  214 Park Ave. — 3rd fl.
  873-7645 (9-5)
  Jell's doctor. $25/hr.

- Dr. Jane Hausman
  830 West Street
  966-4059
  friend of Dr. Johnson's
  (fee?)

- Dr. Peter Devine
  Freeman Clinic
  10-3 Saturdays.
  1004 5th Ave.
  Bill H. went to group here.

- Dr. J. Levmh
  642 Spencer St.
  729-7188
  Paul's dr. 20-30/hr.

Feel free to observe and to ask questions during that first visit:

Where was the analyst trained? You want to make sure that this individual has had a good academic background and is not a charlatan. If the training was at a respectable university and a qualified analytic school, you know that the analyst is at least qualified in terms of education.

What is the approach? Does he or she work on the problems you're facing now or is there an attempt to trace the origins to your childhood? You can ask the value of this particular analyst's method, and decide if that's the route you want to go.

Does this person make sense to you, or do you feel lost in a sea of psychoanalytic doubletalk? You want someone you can easily understand, who speaks plain English and doesn't use a lot of technical terms.

Does this person talk to you or is he or she very quiet? Analysts used to say very little, but today it is considered more beneficial to communicate with the patient.

If the analyst is a man, and you're a woman, does he have a liberated view of women? You don't want to get stuck with someone who has stereotype ideas of a woman's role.

Is the analyst maternalistic or paternalistic? Even though you are in despair, you want to be treated as an equal. You are not there to be babied. Your goal is to learn how to handle your problems. That doesn't mean that you don't want and need compassion, but most of all you need to be treated as a capable adult.

Don't settle on an analyst because he or she is the least expensive. You need competent help, not a bargain.

Once you have selected an analyst you will probably see that person anywhere from once a week to three or four times a week. Once or twice is most common. The analytic hour usually lasts from forty-five to fifty minutes. If the person you have selected dismisses you after forty minutes, or talks on the phone during your session, find someone else. You are paying for uninterrupted time and you have a right to get it.

On the other hand, be wary of the individual who gives you a lot of overtime. There is something indulgent and not very professional about that. Don't allow yourself to be flattered by the extra time. It's probably not for your benefit anyhow. The more equal the relationship, the better off you are.

If after several months you feel you are not making any progress, you should discuss this with the analyst. If he or she tells you that you're very resistant to being helped, and the analyst is having a hard time with you, ask for an explanation. Don't accept an impatient dismissal of your request. You have a right to understand what is going on in your analysis. You may be satisfied with the answer you get but if you're not, and you suspect that the analyst is just making excuses for his or her ineptitude, think about finding someone else. It is annoying to start over again but if you are getting nowhere with this person you owe it to yourself to try someone else.

The tendency, when you have emotional problems, is to turn yourself over to the professional problem solver, but that is not how a satisfactory analysis is achieved. You must play an equal part in this endeavor, for the fact is any changes that are made will be made by you. The analyst is simply there to help you understand what is going on with you, and to guide you toward different behavior.

Psychoanalysis is not some miracle process that will wipe out all problems. Problems are part of the human condition. However, if it is effective (and there's no guarantee it will be effective) it can diminish anxiety and it can help you behave in ways that are productive for you and not destructive. But the effort has to come from you and it has to be continuous. Be suspicious of people who claim to have changed overnight due to some fantastic analyst, or to some new movement that is currently in vogue. People can change but it is a slow process requiring a great deal of energy and thought.

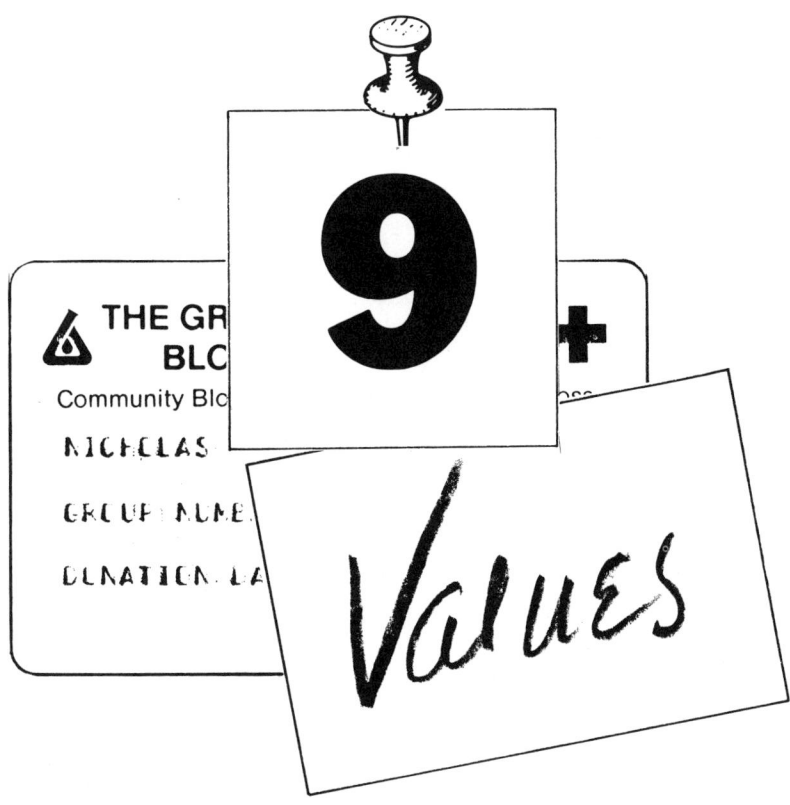

9 Values

So far you have been concentrating on establishing yourself in some very concrete ways—where to live, finding a job, how to handle your money, and how to take care of your health needs. Now you can begin to focus on your values. That may seem like a strange thing to think about, and, in fact, very few people ever address themselves to the subject. Yet, if you want to have control over your life in a meaningful way, you have to come to terms with how you plan to behave in relation to other people. How honest do you want to be? What things are important to strive for?

As you all know only too well, honesty and concern for others have a low priority rating in our society. From the heads of government on down, the approach is often to take what you can get, and to let other people fend for themselves. Most people demonstrate this attitude in small ways: being nice to someone not out of genuine good feelings but to get a favor from them; stealing from the stockroom at work; stealing from motels and restaurants; pocketing money when a person mistakenly gives them too much change; spreading gossip about someone; taking a small bribe in exchange for doing something that is distasteful and perhaps dishonest.

These sound like minor vices, and indeed you could probably indulge in them with few consequences —perhaps a slight twinge of remorse from time to time, or a bit of embarrassment if you are ever found out. The question is: Do you want to be a selfish and dishonest person, even on a small scale? The other question is: How much are you really gaining from the petty thievery and from manipulating people?

Only you can answer the first question, but the answer to the second one is not very much. In fact, you may actually be doing yourself a disservice. For example, it is true that you save some money by lifting rubber bands, paper clips, scissors, note pads, and so forth from the company stockroom, and you can even justify your pilferage by saying that it's a big company with lots of money so nothing will really be missed. That may or may not be true. If every employee steals, it could make a dent in the company funds. But that is not the main point. What is important is how you view yourself. By continually stealing, you are saying that you don't have to abide by rules. You don't have to respect other people's possessions. You are also saying that you have little respect for your own abilities. You see yourself as a person who has to steal. The more you do it the more ingrained the attitude will be. You are saying that you are a person who isn't able to provide for your own needs. You'd be far better off, in terms of your self-esteem, to make a decision to buy the things you can afford and to do temporarily without those things that are too expensive.

Some people steal from work because they feel

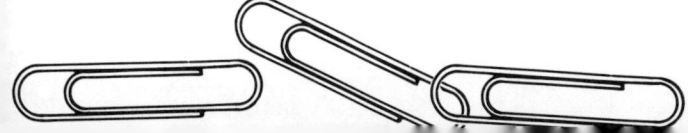

they are being underpaid. They want some fringe benefits as well as a means of getting back at the boss. This is also counterproductive. If you are underpaid, ask for a raise. If it is denied, look for a higher-paying job where you won't feel taken advantage of. By wasting your energies trying to retaliate to a demeaning employer, you allow yourself to wallow in a situation that does you absolutely no good. In every instance, the key to your behavior to others is how you value yourself.

Are you willing to curry favor with someone because they have money or power? Why not earn your own money, and acquire your own strengths, instead of leaning on someone else?

Are you willing to be the recipient of a bribe? Bribes are most often payment for a dishonest action—something the other person knows you won't feel good about doing. Stick with your feelings and keep away from bribes. If you need money, go earn it. Don't become a person who can be bought or sold.

What are you gaining by divulging someone's secrets in the form of gossip? Is your life so paltry that you have to use another individual to make yourself interesting? If so, you'd best make some changes in yourself and leave the reputations of others alone.

It is important not only to respect other people, but also to have a real sense of yourself—a pride in being able to take care of your needs without having to behave in a demeaning fashion, or without finding it necessary to hurt someone else in the process.

After all this discussion, some of you may still decide that it is perfectly okay to pilfer that ashtray, or to go against your conscience for a favor or for financial gain. That's up to you. Just be aware that in the long run you stand to lose more than you'll gain.

You might also give some thought as to how materialistic you want your life to be. There's a big push in our country for everyone to desire the newest car, the

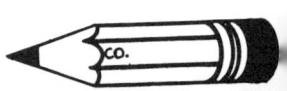

latest clothes, the current makeup, the most modern household appliances. The implication is that one gets status from all these material possessions. Of course that is all nonsense. The consumer doesn't gain real status (maybe some imagined status), but the manufacturer of these products does get rich.

Some people dedicate themselves to the acquisition of material possessions because they don't know what else to strive for. No one wants an aimless life, and the accumulation of things gives an illusion of activity and purpose. The unfortunate part of the pursuit is that it is never totally satisfying; the producers of goods don't want you to feel you ever have enough, so they constantly bring out newer products which make the ones you already have look obsolete. It's a never-ending struggle to keep up, and a very expensive one to boot.

So before you become entangled in the acquisitions game, think about other ways of directing your energies that could give more lasting satisfactions. Find things that are durable and won't go out of style with the next season. This is not an easy thing to do, and you may have to reappraise continually what is really important and valuable to you, but it is worth the time. There's nothing worse than that vague, discontented feeling about one's life—a sense that all is not quite right—without a real understanding of what's bothering you.

The people with whom you choose to associate also come under the heading of values. There are individuals who fill up their lives with friends, simply to keep themselves from feeling lonely. They may not even like most of their so-called friends, but they feel compelled to keep them around. Frequently they are impatient with these people, wishing they would change and become more likeable.

What you must realize is that most people don't change in very profound ways. They may make surface alterations in their lifestyle, but their ingrained patterns of behavior remain the same. The chances are, if you don't like someone today, you won't feel any more kindly disposed toward him or her a year from now. So you must decide how valuable your time is. Do you want to spend long hours with someone you don't much like? Maybe time alone would be more productive.

The important point is to think about your values rather than automatically assuming that what you want, or what you should do, is based on another person's values. That can be hard, and even isolating, especially when you're on your own in a strange town with only your judgment to rely on. Peers might chide you for being cautious or overly honest—"You can do it," they say. "You don't have your mother and father watching over you now."

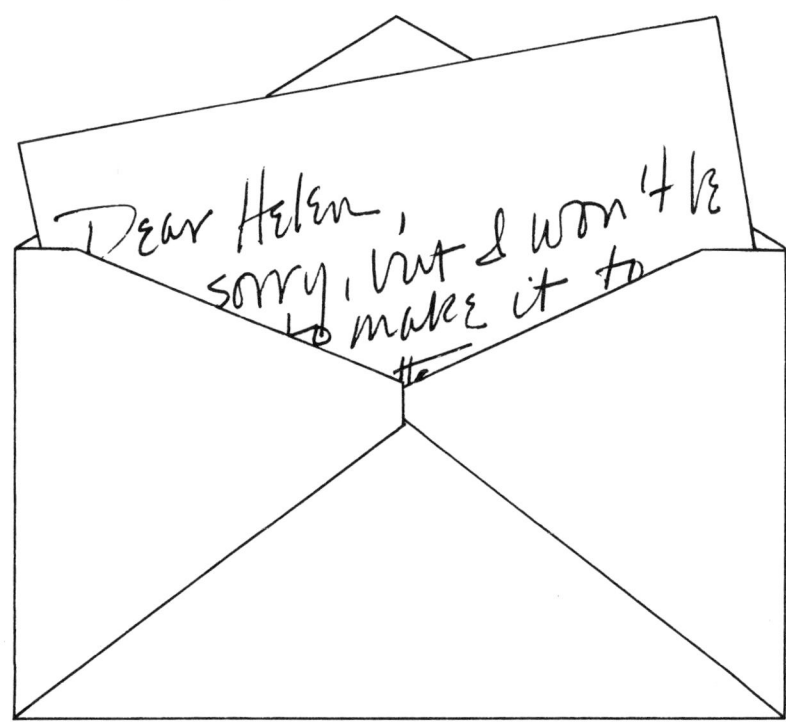

Of course that's true. In the past you could say, "My dad won't let me," when in fact you didn't want to do something. It was comforting to know you had someone to lean on. Independence means standing alone. **You** make the decisions, and that's not easy.

Yet, no matter how difficult it is, stick with your own feelings. If you don't, you'll feel uncomfortable about yourself, as though you have no real control over your own person.

There's one last point to bear in mind: a life built on lies, deceptions, and the pursuit of superficial goals has a very flimsy foundation, and there's always the danger of it collapsing totally. Make your life of stronger stuff. Give it a structure that can withstand a fair amount of turbulence. The adult world is a place of many ups and downs and you'll need something solid to hold onto.

10 Relationships

As an adult your relationships with the opposite sex will probably take on a greater seriousness than they have in the past. Many of you will be thinking of marriage, so each new affair becomes a prospective lifetime commitment. Others, while not eager for a marital partner, might still desire a relationship that offers more than a brief fling at intimacy.

Whatever your goal, be advised that relationships are not easy. Too often the assumption is that once you meet **the** right person your troubles are over. You will love each other and share interests and activities, and all will be right with the world.

Regrettably, it does not work that way. It is true you may care for each other, and there can be some sharing, but there will also be conflicts of interest, a need to raise one's self-esteem at the expense of the other, and a lot of ingrained habits that work against a reasonably agreeable relationship.

If you wish to avoid the constant disappointment over a love affair gone sour, you had better approach your relationships with as much practicality and realism as possible—a hard thing to do because falling in love propels one into a state of rose-colored euphoria.

Your first step is to see the other person as he or she really is, rather than as your perfect fantasy figure. When people are eager to become involved with someone they tend to overlook qualities in the other person that are not to their liking. But ignoring something does not make it disappear, and eventually when the disliked quality becomes so apparent that it must be confronted, the feeling is that the loved one has changed for the worse. The fact is the person didn't change, it's just that he or she was never perceived in a realistic way in the first place.

Your second step is to present yourself as you really are. That is difficult because when you care for someone you want them to think of you as better than all others. No one can blame you for being on your best behavior, but to pretend you're someone you're not is asking for trouble. Keeping up a pretense puts a terrible strain on you, and the other person is never totally deceived—there's always a sense that something about you is not quite honest. In addition, you begin to feel resentful that the real you is not loved; since you've never shown the real you, how can it be? So try to be as much yourself as possible from the start. It will make things a lot easier in the long run.

Perhaps one of the most debilitating problems in a relationship is when one or both people become very dependent on the other. Then, instead of two free individuals getting together because they genuinely like each other, you have two people locked in a relationship out of loneliness or low self-esteem. To avoid such a situation, try to make as much of your own life as possible. If you have a job that pleases you, friends you enjoy, outside activities that keep you involved, you won't feel compelled to lean so heavily on the other person. It is extremely important to have an independent lifestyle so you are not always waiting for the other person to make life entertaining for you. It is also vital that you have a sense of your own worth and are not incessantly demanding that your lover bolster your ego with compliments and assurances of his or her love. That can get wearying. The most durable relationships consist of two equals—a man and a woman who have the strength to be on their own and can maintain that strength as part of a couple.

If you can function independently, you will be comfortable about allowing some degree of privacy to the other person and to yourself. Most people like time alone, but if you're very clutchy in a relationship you'll probably be afraid to say you want some private time for fear the other will feel rejected, or you might be apprehensive of what your lover will do if you're not around. Yet it is important to have time alone in order to reflect, or simply to pursue some special interests that are not shared with the other person. Some people need only a few hours of solitude, while others have to get away alone for a few days. There are relationships that require a lot of togetherness, and there are some that thrive on frequent separations. Discover what is best for you and your partner and act accordingly. There are no laws that say that couples must do **everything** as a team, so you can make your own rules.

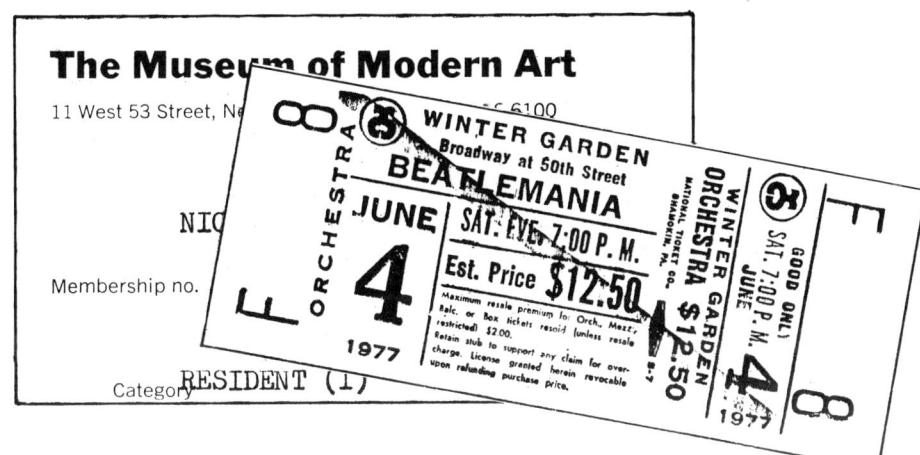

August 1977

Sunday	Monday	Tuesday	Wednesday	Thursday	Friday	Saturday
	1	2 ART CLASS	3	4	5. Movie @ Bob	6
7	8 Concert @ Bob	9 ''	10 Bob–Ball Game Me–Opera	11	12	13 Picnic @ F & G
14	15	16 ''	17	18 Museum Bob @ Guys	19	20
21	22	23 ''	24	25	26 Weekend at Home	27
28 →	29	30	31			

In fact, the more you trust your feelings in a relationship, the better the relationship. Television and films often portray perfect couples who always have common interests and common thoughts. Anything short of the ideal is considered undesirable, or somehow an aberration. Many a real-life relationship has gone aground trying to live up to the myths of the media. Being part of a couple is complicated, and you will experience many differences. That doesn't imply that you should be in a continual argument, but it does mean that if one person doesn't like music and the other does, it is not the end of the world. There are solutions: the person who doesn't like music can try to understand it and enjoy it; the one who likes music can go to concerts with other people, or can even go alone. If music is something so important to one person's life, and the joy can't be shared, it may indeed put a strain on the relationship. If the strain becomes too intense, it could precipitate a break-up. Unfortunately, things don't always work out just the way we want them to. This is just one example, but it can be applied to other aspects of a love affair.

Even if you share many interests, if you don't have mutual respect, you're in trouble. You can disagree, fight, and occasionally hurt one another, but if there's true respect between you, you can survive the difficulties. Respect results from shared values. If you're scrupulously honest and the other individual is in the habit of trying to put one over on everybody, it's going to be hard for you to have much respect for that kind of behavior. You do not have to have every interest in common, but it is vital to have parallel values.

You also must trust one another. To be ever wary of someone you love will cause you pain and a feeling of inequality. You want to feel free to say what's on your mind, to know the other person is comfortable being straight with you. Lack of trust can really kill a relationship. If you are bottling everything up because you sense that opening yourself to the other would expose you to ridicule or cruelty, you'd best do some serious thinking about why you're hanging on to this person who can't be trusted.

Which brings us to a final point: it is almost harder to get out of a relationship than it is to get into one.

There's the worry that the other person will be hurt beyond repair, or the fear that maybe you'll have regrets once you've split up. Well, you've only one life to live, and if you cling to a relationship that is painful or boring or irritating, for whatever reasons, you're wasting your precious time. He or she may be devastated for awhile, but ultimately will recover. You might have some pangs of remorse because you are no longer part of a couple, but it is better to be alone than to spend hours with someone you don't care for. Too many relationships drag on because it seems easier to stick it out than to go through the hassle of making a break. Unfortunately it never really is easier. There you are mired in an unpleasant situation either pretending that it is not bad, or going through miseries because you can't summon the courage to do something decisive. But the longer you put off making a break, the harder it becomes to actually do it. Better to confront the situation and to take some steps as soon as you realize you want out.

Of course it could be the other person who wants out while you would like to continue the relationship. If he or she is serious about wanting the break, you ought to allow it to end. It may be painful initially, but it will be worse to stay with someone who no longer loves you. Just remember, even very intense pain ultimately passes.

Once a relationship is over, try to learn from the mistakes you made before jumping into another love affair. The more you understand your mistakes the less likely you are to repeat them the next time around.

COPING WITH PARENTS

Sue loves her job, but her mother tells her she should be making more money.

Alan likes to work with his hands. His father is pushing him to be an accountant.

Janet, an only child, is building a career. Her parents want her to get married and give them grandchildren.

Joyce's mother criticizes her apartment every time she comes to visit.

Stuart's parents criticize his girlfriends.

Mark's mother complains that he doesn't come to dinner often enough.

Not all parents are critical and complaining. Many encourage their sons and daughters to pursue the things that give them pleasure. But there are cases, like those illustrated above, where parents still try to exert some control over their children's lives, to influence them even after they have become adults. When that happens, it can present a terrible dilemma; you want to be kind to your parents, yet if your life is to have any meaning at all, you must make your own decisions and seek your own goals.

The question is how to look after your interests without hurting your parents. Sometimes it just cannot be done.

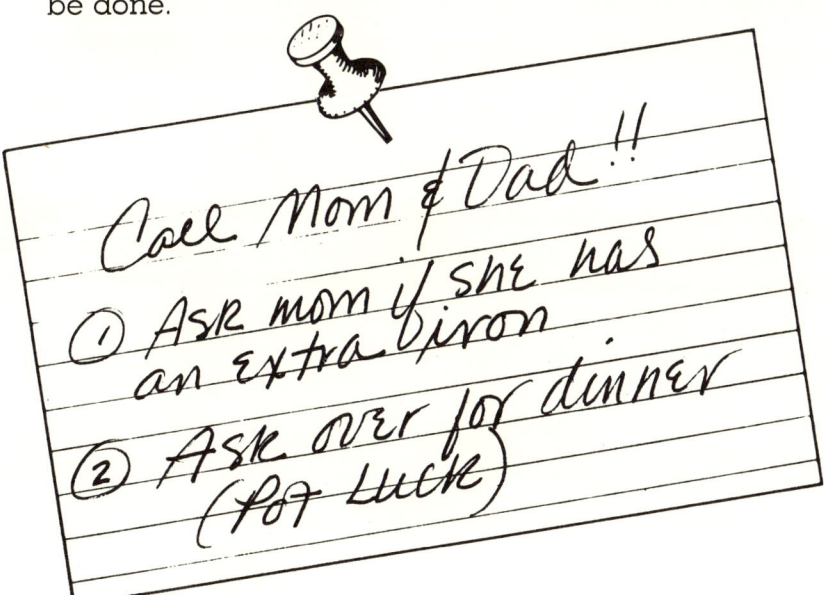

Call Mom & Dad!!
① Ask mom if she has an extra iron
② Ask over for dinner (Pot Luck)

Janet, who wants a career, found that she had to stop communicating with her parents for a while. "First I moved to another city," she relates. "The job opportunities were better, but also I didn't have to hear my folks tell me how selfish I am, that I'm their only hope for ever having grandchildren and I'm letting them down. But even the distance didn't help. They bombarded me with phone calls and letters, and finally I let them know that I didn't want to hear from them. I had to do it at this point because every letter and conversation was really getting me down. Maybe someday, when I feel stronger, we'll be friends again, but for now I must look out for myself."

Alan, on the other hand, continues to see his mother and father. "My dad is still pushing for me to go to college and to get a degree in accounting, but I don't let it upset me," he confides. "I like doing carpentry, and I know it's right for me. I just figure one of these days my father will come round to my way of thinking. But even if he doesn't, I don't care. I'm the one who's living my life, not him."

"My solution," confides Joyce, "is not to have my mother come to my apartment anymore. I used to clean like crazy every time she was to come to dinner, and still she'd find something to criticize. Now we meet for lunch, or I go to her house for dinner. It makes me a little sad not to be able to have her visit me, but it's not worth the hassle."

As you can see, there is no formula for handling parents. Each person has to find his or her own way. Nevertheless, there are things you can think about when your parents start putting uncomfortable pressure on you that will help you decide exactly what you want to do.

● If you are going to function effectively in the adult world, you are going to have to make your own decisions rather than letting others make them for you.

> Wed—
> Dear Mom & Dad —
> I really had a great time coming home last weekend — especially since dad let me win at tennis so easily — (Want another game?) Anyway, I was wondering if the two of you would like to visit me in two

- Even if you make a mistake, it is your mistake and you will learn from it. If you do what your parents insist on, and it does not work out, you will end up being furious and resentful, and feeling very helpless.
- People who want to control your life—and that includes your parents—are thinking of their own needs, not yours.
- Parents are not as fragile as some would have you think. They will not fall apart if you follow your own goals.

- If you want independence, you must give your parents independence as well. This means that you must give up dependent actions such as asking your parents to pay your car insurance, or bringing your laundry home for your mother to wash.
- There is no law that says you have to like your parents, and you should not feel guilty if you decide that you don't like them. You may feel better about your relationship with your parents if you try to look at them as objectively as you do other people, then decide whether they are people you would opt to have as friends. But this is a two-way street, and you must be prepared for your parents to decide that they love you because you are their child, but they simply do not like the person **you** have turned out to be.
- While you may decide that the bad things in your relationship with your parents outweigh the good and you never want to see them again, many people find that the sense of history and roots that they get from a continued relationship with their parents is extremely valuable. If this is the way you feel yet the relationship with your parents is full of stress, consulting with a counselor or a therapist might be helpful in sorting out the situation so that you can keep both your parents **and** your independence.
- While it is true that you are going through a lot of difficulty establishing yourself as an adult, recognize that your parents are going through a lot of changes too. Some parents are reluctant to see their child grow up, because it represents an undeniable proof of the fact that the parents are growing old.
- If you can do so without feeling angry or resentful, try to allay your parents' fears about your ability to take care of yourself. You might do this by trying to act in a more responsible way while you are still living at home. After all, there is no rational reason to expect the parents of an immature, spoiled teen-ager not to be

afraid. In reality, such a teen-ager is in for some hard knocks from the adult world.

● Sometimes parents stay involved in their children's lives because unconsciously the young people want it that way. If you feel that your mother and father are standing at your shoulder, breathing down your neck, you might ask yourself if you are keeping them there, and if you have been unwilling to separate yourself and to stand alone. Think about the following questions:

Do you always ask your parent's advice and then get furious when they give it?

Do you complain to your parents that you are having a hard time, thus bringing them into all your problems?

Do you tell your parents about things you are doing that you know they will disapprove of?

Do you try to convert your parents to your philosophies and attitudes even though it always leads to horrendous arguments?

Whether it's your parents doing the involving, or whether it's you (most often it's both), you can begin to change things. It may mean moving to another city —sometimes just a few miles helps—or it might simply entail letting your folks know that there are certain things you just don't want to discuss, and either they abide by those rules or you will not be able to see them.

Some of you might have to break off the relationship altogether, while others can work things out by not soliciting parental advice. If you are like Stuart, and you find that your folks never care for the people you are intimately involved with, you can simply stop introducing your friends to your parents.

Whatever you do, your goal should always be toward your own independence and autonomy. Parents were necessary to you in the growing-up-years, but as an adult you should no longer be dependent upon them for survival. Now you can, and absolutely should, take care of yourself. If your parents are willing to recognize that, and to respect you and your lifestyle, that is terrific. Then there is a basis for a real friendship. If not, disentangle yourself from them in whatever way you think best, and move forward on your own.

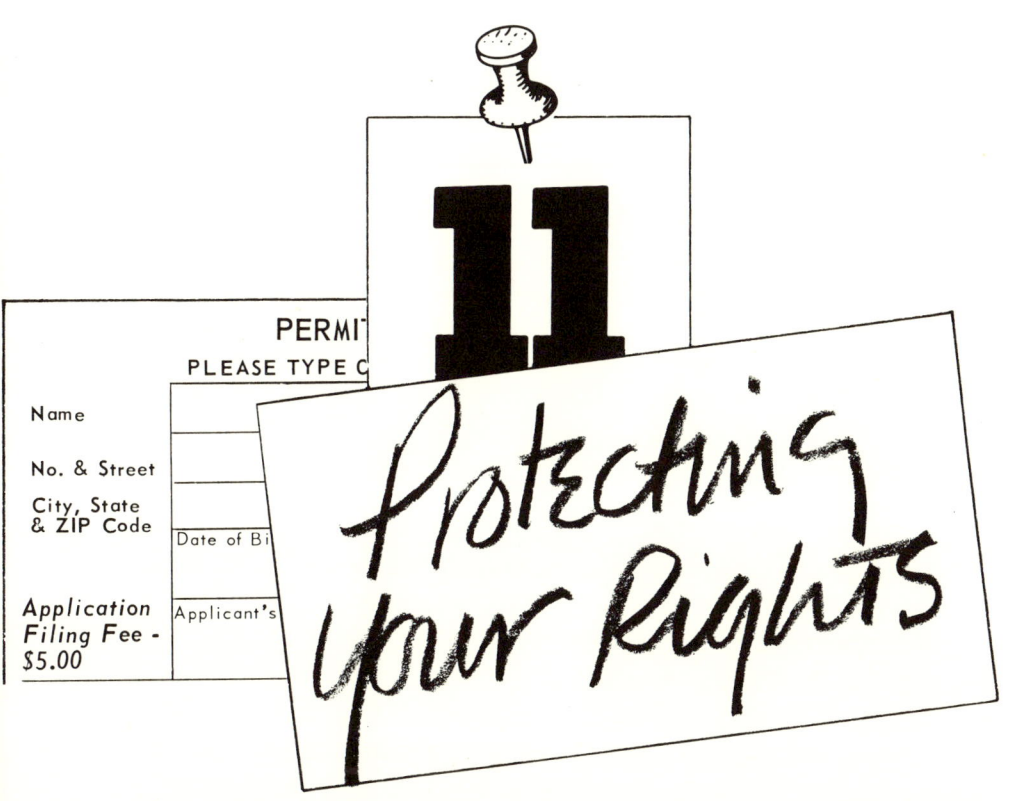

11
Protecting your Rights

As a young person, dependent on parents, you had very few responsibilities toward protecting your rights. If something happened to you, your mother and father were responsible for setting things right. As an adult, the burden is on you. Fortunately, there are many ways of looking after your own best interests, either as an independent person, with legal assistance, or through political channels.

Even if you must resort to the courts, there are some lower courts that will hear small cases without requiring legal representation. If you require counsel, there are organizations such as the Legal Aid Society to provide you with free lawyers. If civil rights are involved, the American Civil Liberties Union will take up the cudgels for you.

It is important that you take your rights seriously. If all people assert themselves when they have been

> *Write to complain about wallet. Stand up for my rights!!*

cheated, harassed, or deprived of what is rightfully theirs, they force business people, corporations, landlords, and government to be honest in their negotiations with individuals.

When dealing with a company, always appeal to the most highly placed person—usually the president. For example, if you purchase something at a department store and it proves defective, you can first try to return it to the salesperson. If for some reason you are refused an exchange or a refund, don't stand around arguing; ask to speak to the manager. If the manager also refuses, and you know your complaint is legitimate, go home and write a letter to the president of the company. Only high officials in an organization have any real power. Type the letter, if possible, and state your complaint very clearly. If you don't know the president's name, simply address your letter to "the President." Explain that you have been a good customer of the store (if this is the first time in the store, tell the president that this was your first purchase and you are shocked by the treatment you received) and that you plan to continue your patronage in the future if the defective item is either exchanged for cash or for a new and perfect item. You can compose your own letter or word it much like the following:

Jane Smith
1014 John Street
Los Angeles, California
734-9056
July 10, 1976

The President
Hunts Department Store
777 Robertson Boulevard
Los Angeles, California
Dear Sir or Madam,

    On July 8 I purchased a wallet for $20.00 from your store. When I got home I noticed the stitching along the bottom was loose, and I realized that the wallet would start to come apart very soon. On July 10 I returned the wallet to the salesperson who had sold it to me and asked to have it exchanged. The salesperson accused me of being careless with the wallet and thus loosening the stitches. An exchange or a refund was refused. The manager also denied my request for the store to make good on the defective wallet. Both the salesperson and the manager were rude and disagreeable, and both blamed me for the loose stitching.

    I have been a reliable customer of Hunts for three years, and I look forward to dealing with your store in the future. Unfortunately, I will be forced to take my business elsewhere if I don't get a new wallet or a cash refund.

    Thank you for your attention.

                      Yours truly,

Be sure you put your name, address, and phone number in the upper right-hand corner so you can be contacted. If you have a charge account with the store, mention that in your letter and say you won't pay for the item until the store makes the necessary adjustments. As a rule, a letter to the president will get the desired action. If it doesn't, and the purchase is under $1000 (the amount may vary from state to state), you can bring an action against the store in Small Claims Court, and you don't have to hire a lawyer. You can also report the store to the Better Business Bureau, which will investigate the matter.

All states have courts that are classified as people's courts. If you have a complaint because of money owed you, someone harassing you, or difficulties with your landlord, you can go to the appropriate court for satisfaction.

States and cities also have agencies to protect your rights. In Chapter 3 you read about using a human rights commission to gain protection against racial, religious, or sex discrimination in housing. But such an agency is active in any complaint involving human rights. There are other agencies that govern health problems—for example, a health hazard in your apartment house—harassment difficulties, noise or air pollution, consumer complaints, and of course the police are available to control crime.

Going through agencies and courts can be time consuming and boring, but if you think you have a case against someone, follow it through. You will be amazed how much stronger you will feel. In addition, you'll gain the respect of the person, or persons, you're bringing action against, and you're less likely to be taken advantage of in the future.

Another avenue of help is through your elected local leaders. You can find out who to talk to by consulting your neighborhood Democratic or Republican Club.

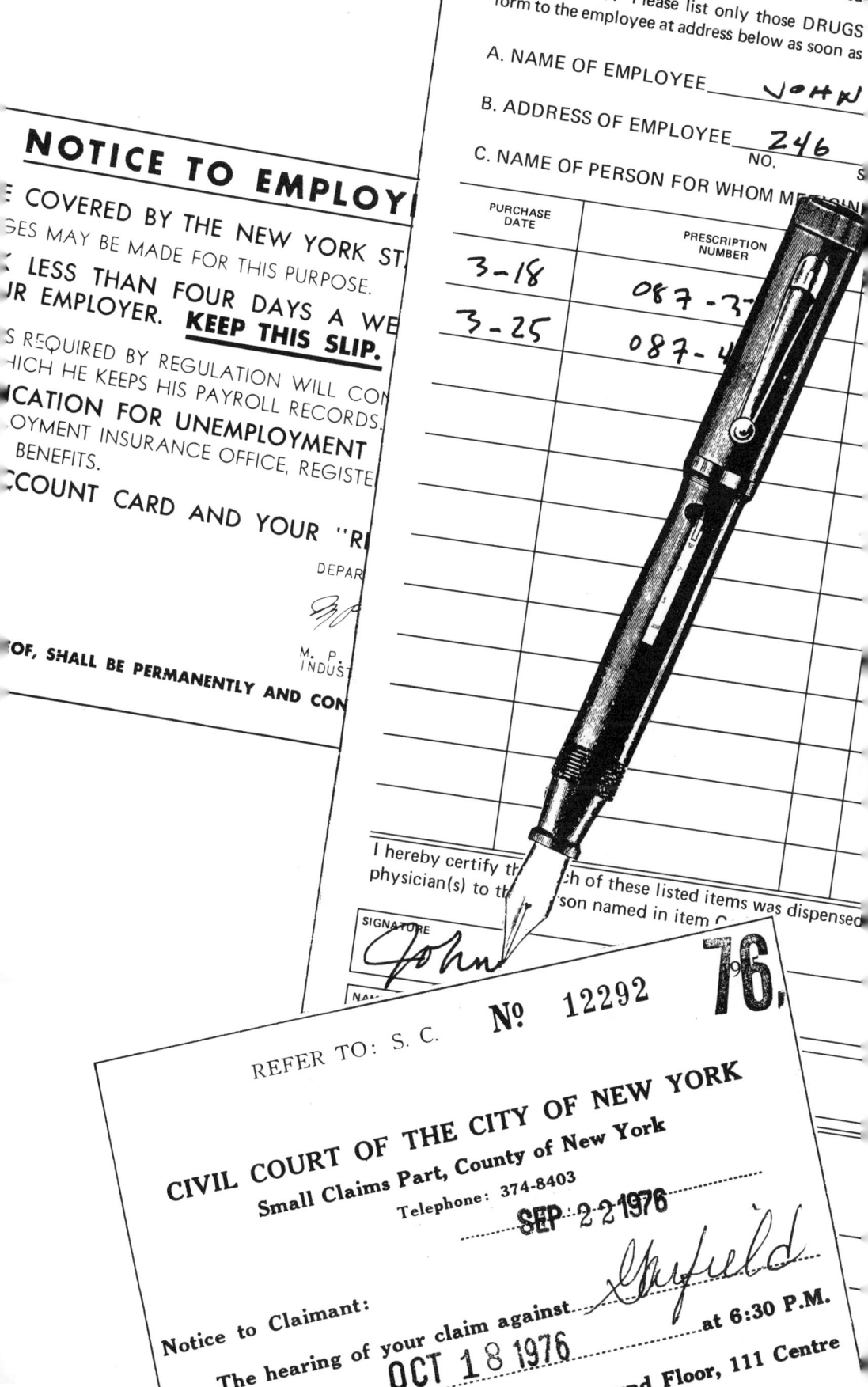

[106]

CUSTOMER'S RECEIPT
NOT NEGOTIABLE

№ 3836

Name: Mrs B. Walker Value 100
Address: 788 Columbus

"Food at"

CARNEGIE
Delicatessen & Restaurant

854 SEVENTH AVENUE
NEW YORK, N. Y.
Between 54th & 55th Sts.

1-3 19 77

Apt.

11 60

Pd

Guest Check

539023

Date	Server	Guests	Table

BRISK

2 10

2 10

Tax
Total

ThankYou

PRINTED IN U.S.A.
REORDER STYLE NO. 1810

NK YOU

Occasionally we are the cause of our own victimization. This can occur from carelessness—not fully reading a contract or warranty, for instance. If we had taken the time, we would have found out that an item was not returnable after ninety days, or a deposit wasn't refundable. In such cases we have no one to blame but ourselves, and there's really nothing that can be done except to learn from the experience.

Never be afraid to take time with anything that affects you. When the bill is presented to you at a restaurant, add it up yourself, and if it's incorrect call it to the waiter's attention. Always count your change—you should even count the money given to you by bank tellers. Tellers, waiters, and salespeople are human beings, and therefore subject to human error.

One of the most effective ways of ensuring your rights is through political action. Although they may seem very remote, the people who serve in the federal government have an impact on what goes on in your community. As an adult, you are able to vote, and even if you haven't reached the voting age you can work for legislation that will be beneficial to you and to the things you believe in. In this age of mind-boggling bureaucracy, it doesn't seem that you are being listened to, but the truth is you are. Elected officials must be responsive to the people who put them in office or they won't be reelected. Letters to senators, congresspersons, and the president are given consideration in the decision-making process. Working with your political club on a more intense level has even more impact.

If the federal government seems too unwieldy and distant, address your efforts to local problems—even if they are as small as getting the sidewalk repaired in front of your house. How a government deals with little problems is indicative of how well it does on larger issues.

When you reach voting age, by all means exercise your right to vote. Do not overlook seemingly unimportant local elections. Do not take the attitude that your vote is meaningless. Every vote is counted, including yours. Your candidate may not be the winner every time, but that's part of life. The minority often becomes the majority in a different election year.

What it all boils down to is that protecting your rights means being active on your own behalf. No one else but you can watch out for your best interests. You need not be a victim in the adult world if you are willing to expend time and energy protecting what's legally yours.

(SIGNATURE OF VOTER

IMPORTANT

You are permanently registered as long as you live at your present address and vote at least once at any General Election held within two calendar years.

If you move from your present address you must re-register in order to be eligible to vote.

12
Extracurricular Activities

Keeping life from becoming an endless routine is much more difficult as an adult than it is as a young person in school. School gives you a variety of classes—it forces you to read, to listen to music, and to participate in art classes. It also gives you sports programs. In the workaday world you will have to find these activities for yourself.

One of the hardest activities to continue, especially if you live in a big city, is athletics, yet it's one of the most necessary. Once you reach your maximum height the only way to grow is in width, which means you will get fat if you don't make some effort to stay in shape. In addition, unexercised muscles, including the heart, lose their firmness, tone, and elasticity. So get into the habit of exercising regularly, while you're still young, and you won't be faced with a plump, unbending, flabby body by the time you're thirty.

THE EXERCISE HABIT

Answer the following questions:

Which would you choose, a chance to walk or a chance to ride?

Would you rather play a sport or watch others play?

When you think of relaxing, do you think of watching television?

Do you get some exercise at least two or three times a week?

Answers:

If you have the exercise habit, you would:

Walk rather than ride.

Play a sport rather than watch.

You probably average only about an hour of TV a day.

You exercise at least twice a week.

Get in shape and stay in shape. It's good for the mind and body!

There are many ways of staying in condition: you can play basketball, handball, volleyball, or squash two or three times a week. Bowling is good for the waist if done more than once a week. Jogging several times a week is inexpensive and good for you (don't overdo). Tennis is very popular but very expensive in cities. Walking briskly two or three miles a day is excellent exercise. Try walking to and from work. Bicycling to work and back is also good. The trouble is that you are constantly inhaling fumes from cars in front of you and that's not so great for the lungs. Dance classes are wonderful and so is yoga. Yoga exercises every part of the body. Swimming also exercises the entire body and is one of the best ways to stay in shape. If you don't get bored, you can do the Canadian Air Force exercises (available in a paperback book) at home each morning. Or you can do the regular calisthenics such as situps, pushups, jumping-jacks, and so forth.

Find the activity most appealing to you and stick with it. Once a week is not enough. Classes should be attended two or three times a week, and exercises should be done every day—ten minutes a day is better than two hours once a week.

But don't stop with your body. Keep your mind in shape too. Avoid the habit of plunking yourself down in front of a television every evening. Patronize your local library so you have something to read. Get involved with activities in the community: local politics; the church; adult education classes; choral groups if you can sing and read music; craft classes if you enjoy working with your hands; a theater group if you like to act or work backstage. Maybe you've always wanted to learn the piano or the guitar. Now is the time to do it.

Traveling is another thing you can do now that you're on your own. It needn't be expensive. Camping trips are fun. Bicycling trips through parts of the United

[112]

States or Europe can be educational, good exercise, and enjoyable. There are all kinds of charter flights to Europe, and a train trip that goes through Canada. Often travel agents can put you onto cheap and interesting travel packages. By the way, you never pay a travel agent a commission. The commission comes from the airlines.

If you want to work and travel, and you can type or take dictation, many temporary employment agencies have branches throughout the United States, and in Canada and England. You are issued a travel service card, or a referral card, from the office in your city which can be presented wherever that service has branches. Temporary secretarial work always seems to be plentiful, even in a depressed economy, so you can be assured of picking up some money should you run short.

Whatever activities you decide to pursue, the choices are numerous. Find things that are interesting and challenging, that bring some vitality to your daily routine. A well-known psychologist was once asked how you can tell what you'll be like when you grow old. "Look at yourself as you are now," he replied. "That's how you'll be when you're older—only more so."

This is a good thought to keep in mind as you begin to mold the many facets of your life.

Index

Adult, definition of, 3
American Civil Liberties Union, 101
Analysts, choosing, 76–82
Apartments, 13–32
    classified ads for, 15–17
    community emergency and, 30
    decorating, 27–28, 32
    furnished, 21
    furniture for, 21–25, 31
    housing discrimination, 18–19
    kitchenware for, 24, 26
    in large cities, 14–15
    leases, 19
    linens for, 24, 26
    neighborhood and, 9–10, 14
    questioning neighbors about, 19
    rental agreement, 17
    renting agents, 17–18
    repairs, 28–29
    roommates and, 14–16
    safety rules in, 10–11
    security deposit, 17
    sublet clause, 19–20
    superintendents, 17
Automobiles
    buying, 50
    insurance coverage, 51

Becker, Marion Rombauer, 58
Beds, 21–22
Better Business Bureau, 104
Bicycling, 111, 113
Blender, 26
Bookcases, 24
Borrowing money, 52
Bribes, 85
Budgeting, 54–56

Calisthenics, 111
Carpenter's claw hammer, 28
Chairs, 21, 22, 23
Character reference, 35
Charge account buying, 48–49
Chests, 23–24

City life, 9–12
Classified ads, 6, 15–17
Companies dealing with, 102–104
Consumer Reports, 26–27
Cookbooks, 58
Coworkers, relations with, 42, 44
Credit, 48–49, 52

Dance classes, 111
Decorating apartments, 27–28, 32
Dentists, choosing, 72–76
Department stores, 21, 24–25
Discrimination, housing, 18–19
Dishes, 26
Doctors, choosing, 67–72
Door locks, 10

Electricity, community emergency and, 30
Employer, relations with, 41–42, 45
Employment. **See** Jobs
Employment agency, 36–40
Exercising, 109–111
Extracurricular activities, 109–113

Firings from jobs, 42
Food, 57–64
    balanced meals, 58–59
    buying tips, 66
    cookbooks, 58
    high calorie, 64
    junk-food habit, 60
    labels, 60
    low calorie, 65
    party, inexpensive, 63
    planning meals, 58–60
    recipes, 58, 60–62
Furnished apartments, 21
Furniture
    buying, 21–25

    manufacturer's label, 31
    unpainted, 34

Gas supply, community emergency and, 30
Goals, long-range, 6–7
Good Cheap Food (Ungerer), 58
Gynecologists, 68

Hammers, 28
Hi-risers, 22
Honesty, 83, 87
Hospitals, 67
Housing discrimination, 18–19
Human rights commission, 18, 104

Independence, 88, 90–92
Installment buying, 48–49
Insurance, automobile, 51
Interest rates, 49, 52
Internists, 68
Interviews, 35–37

James Beard Bread Book, 62
Jobs, 5–6, 33–46
    applications, 38–39
    character reference, 35
    dissatisfaction with, 43
    employment agencies, 36–40
    excessive work, 44
    firings, 42
    honesty and, 46
    interviews, 35–37
    personnel departments, 39
    quitting, 44–45
    raise, requesting, 45
    relations with coworkers, 42, 44
    relations with employer, 41–42, 45
    résumé, 35
    skills and, 6, 38–39

stealing and, 84–85
temporary, 34, 113
training, 34–35
traveling and, 113
women and, 33–34
Joy of Cooking (Rombauer and Becker), 58, 61

Kitchenware, 24, 26

Leases, 19
Legal Aid Society, 101
Linens, 24, 26
Loans, 52
Locks, 10
Lodgings, temporary, 13–14
Love affairs, 89–94

Materialism, 85–86
Mattress
    buying, 21
    maintenance of, 31
Meals. **See** Food
Meat sauce, 60–61
Medical help, 67–82
    analysts or therapists, 76–82
    dentists, 72–76
    doctors, 67–72
Money, 47–56
    borrowing, 52
    budgeting, 54–56
    buying cars, 50
    credit, 48–49, 52
    needs and, 48
    savings, 55

Nails, 28
Neighborhood, choosing, 9–10, 14

Obstetrician-gynecologists, 68
Orthodontists, 75

Parents, relationship with, 94–100

Passbook loan, 52
Personnel departments, 39
Phillips screw driver, 28
Physicians, choosing, 67–72
Political action, 107–108
Psychoanalysts, choosing, 76–82
Psychotherapists, choosing, 76–82
Psychiatric social workers, 77
Psychiatrists, choosing, 76–82

Raises, asking for, 45
Recipes, 58, 60–62
Relationships, 89–100
    coworkers, 42, 44
    employers, 41–42, 45
    opposite sex, 89–94
    parents, 94–100
Rental agreement, 17
Renting agent, 17–18
Repairs, apartment, 28–29
Residence halls, 13
Restaurants, tipping in, 62
Résumé, 35
Rights, protection of, 101–108
    courts and, 101, 104
    dealing with companies, 102–104
    political action and, 107–108
Rombauer, Irma S., 58
Roommates, 14–16

Salvation Army, 22–23
Savings, 55
Screw drivers, 28
Screws, 28
Security deposits, 17
Self-knowledge, 5–7
Sheets, 24–25
Silverware, 26
Skills, 6, 38–39
Small Claims Court, 104
Sofas, 21, 22

Spaghetti sauce, 60–61
Stainless steel flatware, 26
Stealing, 84–85
Sublet clause, 19–20
Superintendents, 17
Swimming, 111

Tables, 23
Tack hammer, 28
Temporary work, 34, 113
Therapists, choosing, 76–82
Tipping, 62
Toaster, 26
Tool chest, 28
Towels, 24–25
Training, 34–35
Travel agents, 113
Traveling, 111, 113

Ungerer, Miriam, 58
Unpainted furniture, 34
Used-furniture, 22–24

Values, 83–88, 93
Vegetarian Epicure, The
   (Thomas), 58

Walking, 11–12, 111
Water supply, community
   emergency and, 30
Window frame decoration,
   32
Window guards, 10
Work. **See** Jobs

YMCA (YMHA), 13
YWCA (YWHA), 13

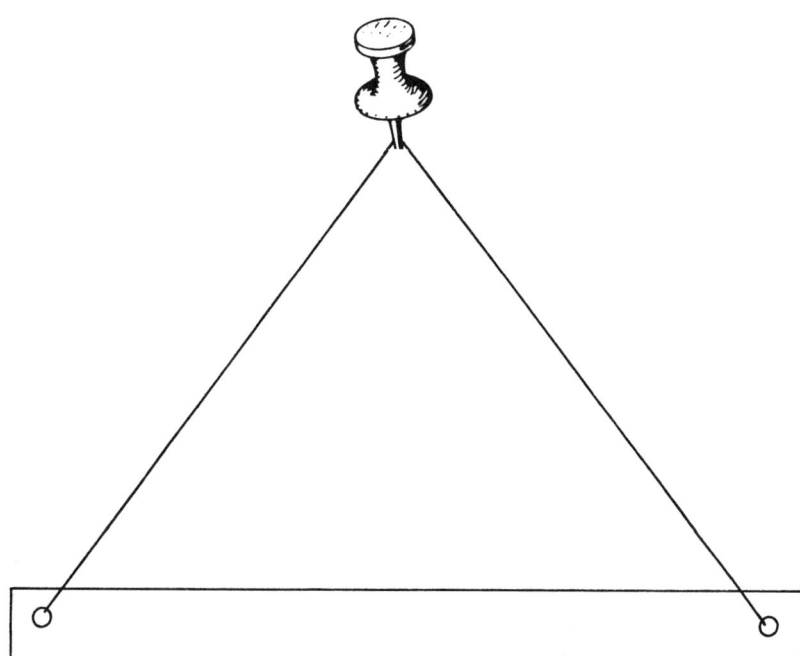

ABOUT THE AUTHOR

Greta Walker, a graduate of U.C.L.A., came to New York from Los Angeles when she was twenty-one years old. In her own words, "The adult world was not easy for me to adjust to. I learned the hard way, and much of the advice I give throughout this book is based on my own mistakes and learning."

Ms. Walker did make it in New York. She was an actress for ten years and appeared in many Broadway and off-Broadway plays as well as in television and summer stock. She studied singing, and still sings lieder and opera arias for her own pleasure.

Her published books include: Women Today: Ten Profiles, published by Hawthorn, and Modeling Careers, A Career Concise Guide, published by Franklin Watts.